THE MAN
MOST LIKELY TO . . .

A Comedy

JOYCE RAYBURN

SAMUEL   FRENCH

LONDON

NEW YORK   TORONTO   SYDNEY   HOLLYWOOD

© 1969 BY JOYCE RAYBURN

ISBN 0 573 01262 8

THE MAN MOST LIKELY TO . . .

Produced at the Vaudeville Theatre, London, on the 4th July 1968, by Sherwood and Reid, and Le Clare Productions, Ltd, with the following cast of characters:

(in order of their appearance)

VICTOR CADWALLADER	*Leslie Phillips*
JOAN CADWALLADER	*Diane Hart*
MARTIN·MORLEY	*Dermot Walsh*
SHIRLEY HUGHES	*Ciaran Madden*
GILES CADWALLADER	*Trevor Kent*

The play directed by LESLIE PHILLIPS

Setting by GEOFFREY SCOTT

SYNOPSIS OF SCENES

The action of the play passes in a week-end cottage in Berkshire

ACT I
Saturday morning

ACT II
Saturday night

(During this act the lights are lowered to denote the passing of 1½ hours)

ACT III
Sunday morning

Time—the present

ACT I

Windows run along the entire back of the room with entrances up R *and* L *which lead out into the garden. There is a swing door up* L *with a large round window in it, which leads to the kitchen. Down* L *are glazed and curtained double doors which lead to the dining-room and upstairs. A large open fireplace with hood dominates the corner down* R. *The room is tastefully furnished.*

As the CURTAIN *rises,* VICTOR *enters through the french windows.*

(JOAN *enters from the kitchen*)

JOAN. Oh, there you are, Victor. Where have you been hiding?

VICTOR (*irritably*) I haven't been hiding. I went for a walk.

JOAN (*moving to the desk*) You should have let us know. Martin would have gone with you. (*She lights a cigarette*)

VICTOR. Exactly. I was thinking something out. I came to a final decision four times.

JOAN. I was like that about lunch. But I've settled for apple crumble.

VICTOR. I hate apple crumble.

JOAN. Giles loves it.

VICTOR. My son will eat anything, won't he.

JOAN (*moving* R *of the chair*) What's the matter with you today? You're in a filthy mood.

VICTOR. Darling, why did we buy this place?

JOAN. For week-ends.

VICTOR. For what at week-ends?

JOAN. Fresh air, mainly.

VICTOR. What else?

JOAN. There's golf.

VICTOR. Yes . . .

JOAN. A nice pub in the village.

VICTOR. What about the original reason—unless of course you've forgotten what it was? I was suffering, if you remember, from nervous tension.

JOAN (*moving up* L) You were suffering, if I remember, from chronic bad temper.

VICTOR. No, that was a surface manifestation. The root cause was tension, and the idea was to come out here, away from town, traffic and telephone, and unwind. Un-bloody-wind.

JOAN. So who's stopping you?

VICTOR. You are. You fill the house from cellar to loft with ghastly people.

JOAN. That's a slight exaggeration, darling.

VICTOR. What about last week-end, then, eh? Laughing George and his dreary wife.

JOAN. They didn't stay long, did they? They left very early on Sunday morning.

VICTOR. Nothing to do with me.

JOAN. No?

VICTOR. Their endless stories, none of which is true. They wouldn't be funny if they were. "You must get George to tell you what happened to him in Oslo."

JOAN. And what did you say?

VICTOR (*moving above the table* C) Why?

JOAN. And the fact that they left early had nothing to do with you.

VICTOR. One little word, "why". Can I help it if they've got no sense of humour?

JOAN. They are getting on, you know.

VICTOR (*wandering down* L) That's very true. Everybody you know seems to have one foot in the grave and the other on our doorstep.

JOAN (*laughing*) Oh, Victor!

VICTOR (*throwing the newspaper on the sofa* LC *and moving above it*) Well, darling, they depress me, they really do—tottering about displaying their infirmities. (*He mimes myopia*) "Where are my glasses, dear?" "On the end of your nose, dear." (*He mimes deafness*) "Where, dear?" Ah, youth, youth! (*He makes a grand gesture and hurts his back*) Ouch! (*He sits on the chaise-longue*)

JOAN (*moving to Victor*) Yes, we all know about you and youth. Your back still troubling you?

VICTOR. A bit.

JOAN. I'll rub some of that stuff on it. (*She rubs his back, then moves away* C *smiling to herself*)

VICTOR. What's so funny?

JOAN (*controlling herself*) Nothing. Anyway you can't complain this week-end. We've only got Martin.

VICTOR. Only! You know exactly what I think of . . .

(MARTIN *enters from the kitchen wearing an apron*)

Hullo, Martin.

MARTIN. Hullo. We've been preparing the fatted calf for the prodigal son. (*He picks up the paper and moves* RC)

VICTOR. You can always be relied on to state the obvious.

JOAN. And peel the apples. And slice the beans and make the gravy . . .

VICTOR. And pinch my paper.

MARTIN. I'm terribly sorry . . .

VICTOR. That's all right.

MARTIN. I enjoy cooking. It keeps me out of mischief. (*He moves* R *of Joan*) Doesn't Joanie look lovely this morning?

VICTOR. My wife always looks good in pink.

JOAN. I'm wearing green.

VICTOR (*noticing for the first time*) Yes. But there's a sort of pinkish tinge to it.

JOAN. You never admit defeat, do you?

VICTOR. My name is Victor.

(MARTIN *and* JOAN *exchange glances*)

MARTIN (*sitting on the stool down* R *and reading the paper*) Well—what's it going to be this time? Repentant son and forgiving father? Or the other way about?

JOAN. Tempers should have cooled on both sides after six months. Six months!

VICTOR. I'd be quite happy to wait another six.

JOAN. Well, I wouldn't. I worry about him—all by himself in Manchester.

VICTOR. Where the natives are known to be dangerous. I should have thought at nineteen he should be quite capable of looking after himself.

JOAN. Giles is very young for his age.

VICTOR. Giles is young for any age.

JOAN. I've been sending him fruit cakes and things.

VICTOR. Why is it that maternal love always expresses itself in terms of high calories?

MARTIN. It's the continuation of giving suck.

VICTOR. Good lord, is it really? (*Rising*) And if I were to offer you a drink?

MARTIN. That's quite different.

VICTOR (*moving to the drinks cabinet*) Oh, I'm so glad. Joan?

JOAN. Not for me, thanks.

MARTIN. I'll have a tiny dry sherry if I may, Victor.

VICTOR. No spirits, eh, Martin? You're very abstemious, aren't you.

MARTIN. I have to be. I don't have your robust constitution.

VICTOR (*crossing to Martin with the sherry bottle and a glass*) I was a premature baby, as a matter of fact. (*He pours sherry for Martin, returns to the drinks table and pours a brandy for himself*) Brought on by a strenuous performance of *The Mikado*. Mum was singing "Three Little Maids from School Are We" when she was struck by a sharpish pain.

MARTIN. And yet you're completely unmusical.

VICTOR. I wouldn't say that. I can sing "Land of Hope and Glory".

JOAN. And make it sound like "Comin' Thro the Rye".

VICTOR. Perhaps you should have got me to do an audition before you married me.

MARTIN. She should have married me.

JOAN (*moving to Martin*) You could be right. But I've kept your friendship, darling, and Victor doesn't mind.

VICTOR (*moving above the chaise-longue to* C) Victor's never been consulted, has he?

JOAN. I hope you're going to be nice to Giles.

VICTOR. Why d'you say that?

JOAN. I shall never forget how you told him that he leapt from failure to failure with the agility of a mountain goat and less intelligence.

VICTOR. Did I really say that?

JOAN. I'm afraid you did.

VICTOR. That's rather neat, isn't it?

JOAN. Very unkind.

VICTOR. Then he must have provoked me, because I'm a kind man, at bottom. (*He sits on the chaise-longue*)

JOAN. You hide it remarkably well.

(MARTIN *sips his sherry cautiously*)

VICTOR. Are you saving the rest of your tiny dry sherry till later, Martin? You'll live to be a great age.

MARTIN. I doubt it.

VICTOR. Yes, you'll live to be a grand old man. I wonder how old one has to be to be a grand old man? Eighty? Ninety?

MARTIN. Yes, I wonder.

VICTOR. You've got a couple of years to go yet. Ladies become wonderful, we become grand. They play records for you on Radio Two.

JOAN. That's something you can look forward to.

VICTOR. Is it really? The joke is, everybody overlooks the worthless life you may have led.

MARTIN. Nobody could call your life worthless, Victor. (*He moves up LC, throwing the paper on the armchair*) You've built up a mighty industrial empire.

VICTOR. One small manufacturing group. Don't turn it into E.M.I.

JOAN. Martin pays you a compliment and you snap his head off.

VICTOR. I'm sorry, Martin.

MARTIN (*moving on to the rostrum*) That's perfectly all right, Victor.

JOAN. He was only trying to be pleasant.

VICTOR. I said I was sorry, didn't I?

MARTIN (*moving* c) Shouldn't Giles be here by now?

JOAN (*linking her arm in Martin's*) Oh, I have missed him.

MARTIN. You've had us.

VICTOR. Us? Is this marriage a partnership or a limited company?

JOAN. There have been times when I've been jolly glad of a second string.

VICTOR. D'you hear that, Martin? You're a second string. Put that on your cello and pluck it.

MARTIN. I've been quite happy to look after Joanie when you've been so terribly busy.

VICTOR (*to Joan*) Have I neglected you, darling?

JOAN. Off and on.

VICTOR. Oh, well, mighty industrial empires don't grow like mushrooms.

MARTIN (*moving to the armchair and sitting*) That's true, but I've always made it a rule never to let my work interfere with my private life. When I shut the office door that's it for the day.

VICTOR. I do hope you're not comparing your job with mine. Nobody would notice if you went to sleep at your desk—as long as you kept your glasses on.

MARTIN. My position at the Ministry happens to be a most responsible one.

VICTOR. You were away for five weeks with a hernia and the country didn't grind to a halt.

MARTIN. It was all waiting for me when I got back.

VICTOR. What was? A gallon and a half of cold tea?

JOAN. Stop bickering, you two.

MARTIN. Victor has great drive and attack. He forges ahead while others hesitate. He sees what he wants and he makes straight for it.

JOAN (*to Victor*) There you are, you see. An unsolicited testimonial.

VICTOR. Yes. I'm waiting for the sting in the tail.

MARTIN. No, no, no. I sincerely admire the qualities in you which I lack. Your initiative. Your enormous self-confidence.

VICTOR. Ah, but you have other qualities, Martin. A subtlety I couldn't acquire in a thousand years. You're trying as always, to make me feel guilty.

MARTIN. Everything I say is suspect.

JOAN (*moving L of the armchair*) That was ungracious of you, Victor.

VICTOR. You know perfectly well he's got a grudge against me, just because he imagines that I pinched his girl.

JOAN (*moving to Martin*) Well, we were engaged.

MARTIN. And the date was fixed.

VICTOR (*going to pour himself another brandy*) Is that any reason to hang around ever since, looking like the loser of the bloodhound section at Cruft's? You could have found someone else, couldn't you?

MARTIN (*taking Joan's hand*) There's only one Joanie.

VICTOR. Yes, and if I were to say, take her, she's yours, you'd be a cloud of dust on the horizon before she had time to say no.

JOAN. What makes you so sure that I would say no?

MARTIN. Or that I'd disappear in a cloud of dust, for that matter?

VICTOR (*moving above the chaise-longue to C*) You'd better watch your step you know, Martin. One day fate might call your bluff.

JOAN. You're so aggressive, Victor.

VICTOR. Me? I'm the meekest and most inoffensive of men! (*He sits on the chaise-longue*)

JOAN. Now that Giles has agreed to come and see us . . .

VICTOR. That's very handsome of him, I'm sure.

JOAN (*sitting on the chaise-longue*) Darling, he's coming all the way from Manchester. Promise me that you'll at least meet him half way.

VICTOR. What—Birmingham?

JOAN. You know perfectly well what I mean. Unbend a little. Try to understand his point of view.

VICTOR. He makes no attempt to understand mine.

MARTIN. Father and son—two stags with their antlers locked in the age-old combat.

VICTOR. Oh, my Gawd!

JOAN. Martin's right. You're both proud and stubborn. But I didn't think you'd drive him out of the house.

VICTOR. I didn't drive him out of the house. He went of his own accord. It was that evening we went out to dinner, don't you remember? And we came back after that awful Chicken Marengo to find an empty nest.

JOAN. I was so upset. I was sick.

VICTOR. You'd have been sick anyway.

JOAN (*rising*) It was your fault he left. (*She moves up* C)

VICTOR. Oh, yes, it was Daddy's fault. It's always Daddy's fault. It was Daddy's fault when he poured his bloody cocoa down my neck.

JOAN. He gave way to an impulse.

VICTOR. A nasty brown impulse.

JOAN. He was only two years old at the time. If you're going to rake up things that happened before he reached the age of reason . . .

VICTOR. As far as I'm concerned he's never reached it. And never will.

JOAN. At least he had the common sense to put two hundred miles between himself and you. (*Suddenly*) The joint!

MARTIN (*rising and moving to the kitchen with the paper*) Leave it to me. I'll baste it.

(VICTOR *signs that he wants the paper back*)

(*Handing Victor the paper*) I'm terribly sorry.

VICTOR. That's quite all right.

JOAN. Bless you, Martin. (*She sits in the armchair*)

(MARTIN *exits to the kitchen*)

VICTOR. That's right. Let Martin do it. He's just the one for ladling spoonfuls of grease. I don't know why I put up with him. Any other husband would have sued him by now for alienation of affection. Why did you have to ask him this week-end, with Giles coming?

JOAN. Because he's very good at filling in awkward cracks in the conversation and smoothing over rough patches.

VICTOR. The complete home decorator. I think I can talk to my wayward son without Martin's slimy support.

JOAN. If you're going to regard Giles as a wayward child, the cause is lost before we start. He's our only child——

VICTOR. No.

JOAN. —and it's thanks to you that I haven't seen him since last autumn. If you don't make peace with Giles, I shall find it very hard to forgive you.

VICTOR (*rising and moving to the window up* L) Yes, I know.

JOAN. And don't go wandering off again. I can never find you. You're for ever lurking in bushes.

VICTOR. Well, we all have our weaknesses. Think of your Uncle Henry.

JOAN. I'd rather not, thank you.

VICTOR. I often wonder what satisfaction he used to get from standing at lighted windows wearing nothing but a crooked smile.

JOAN. Not half as much as you get from constantly reminding me of it.

(MARTIN *enters*)

MARTIN. Everything's under control.

VICTOR. If you'll excuse me, I'll just nip outside—and sharpen my antlers.

(VICTOR *exits to the garden and goes off* R)

JOAN. He's so difficult.

MARTIN (*moving to Joan*) I marvel at your patience.

JOAN. Martin, take that look off your face.

MARTIN. What look?

JOAN. That it-all-could-have-been-so-very-different look. It's getting to be a set expression.

MARTIN. I'm a drag.

JOAN. No, you're not. You know I couldn't have managed without you. Especially at the beginning. He's calmer now—now that he's achieved most of his ambitions.

(VICTOR *appears at the window up* R)

He's bored, I know—but much calmer.

VICTOR. Everything under control.

JOAN (*rising and moving to the kitchen*) Time to set the table.

MARTIN (*picking up the bowl of roses and moving to the kitchen*) Shall we use these for the centre?

JOAN. You have such lovely ideas, Martin.

VICTOR. Oh, my God . . .

JOAN (*to Victor*) You'd never think of a thing like that.

(JOAN *exits to the kitchen*)

MARTIN. Victor has other things on his mind.

(MARTIN *exits to the kitchen*)

VICTOR. Yes. Want any help?

(VICTOR *goes to the drinks and pours himself a brandy. A* GIRL *of about eighteen enters from the window up* R. *She is wearing a leather jacket and flared trousers, and is holding a crash helmet*)

SHIRLEY. Hallo.

VICTOR. Hallo-o?

SHIRLEY. Is any of that for sale?

VICTOR. What would you like?

SHIRLEY. Mind if I mix it myself? (*She starts to take off her jacket*)

VICTOR (*moving* C) No, feel free, feel free.

SHIRLEY (*placing her jacket on the back of the armchair*) You're very kind.

VICTOR. At bottom.

SHIRLEY (*taking off her trousers to reveal a dolly dress*) It's ridiculous, isn't it? The amount of gear you have to swaddle yourself in to keep reasonably warm and clean on the back of a bike.

VICTOR. Yes, it's ridiculous. (*He turns away*)

SHIRLEY. It's all right. You can look.

VICTOR (*turning*) Oh.

SHIRLEY. Did you think I'd forget when to stop?

VICTOR. I thought you might get carried away.

SHIRLEY (*moving to the drinks*) It's awfully warm, isn't it?

VICTOR (*loosening his collar*) Very close, yes.

SHIRLEY (*pouring vodka, gin and lime into a glass*) Don't you want to know who I am? Or do you normally dispense free drinks to anybody who wanders in?

VICTOR. I could never refuse a pretty girl.

SHIRLEY. Oh, I like that. A touch of the old-fashioned gallantry.

VICTOR. It's in short supply now, is it?

SHIRLEY. Bit thin on the ground.

VICTOR. That's the price you pay for equality. That's a curious mixture!

SHIRLEY. It's a combined pick-you-up and lay-you-out.

VICTOR. What's the lime for?

SHIRLEY (*moving* L *of Victor*) To kill the whole disgusting taste.

VICTOR (*amused*) You don't enjoy it, then?

SHIRLEY (*shaking her head*) Purely medicinal. Cheers. (*She drinks*) Ugh! (*Holding out her hand*) I'm Shirley Hughes.

VICTOR (*shaking it*) Victor Cadwallader.

SHIRLEY. I know. Haven't you heard of me? Shirley?

VICTOR. No. Should I have?

SHIRLEY. I thought Giles might have mentioned my name. He does write home occasionally, doesn't he?

VICTOR. So you're a friend of my son's?

SHIRLEY. Don't look so downcast, as if it ruled out all further possibilities.

VICTOR. My dear, the thought never even crossed my mind. I'm too tired for that sort of thing.

SHIRLEY. That wasn't a tired look you gave me when I came in.

VICTOR. Mm. Do sit down. (*He motions to the armchair*)

(SHIRLEY *sits on the rug in front of the fire*)

Did you come down with Giles?

SHIRLEY. Yes. On Elsie.

VICTOR. Who?

SHIRLEY. We call the bike Elsie.

VICTOR. Oh, I see.

SHIRLEY. She conked out back there so I hitched a lift.

VICTOR. Where's Giles then?

SHIRLEY. A couple of miles back. He may have started her by now. She gets overheated.

VICTOR (*moving down* L) I'm not surprised. I'd better nip down in the car and pick him up.

SHIRLEY. You wouldn't do that, would you?

VICTOR. Why wouldn't I?

SHIRLEY. It doesn't fit in with Giles' opinion of you. In fact, you're not at all as he described you.

VICTOR (*moving back to Shirley*) That's just as well, isn't it?

SHIRLEY. It certainly is. I expected you to be pompous and scowling.

VICTOR (*laughing*) That's me, all right.

SHIRLEY. I'd say there was a lot of fun in you. (*She looks at him in a meaningful way*)

VICTOR. Let's talk about the weather now, shall we?

SHIRLEY. It's too late. It's happened.

VICTOR. What has?

SHIRLEY. The spark. Instant ignition.

VICTOR. Some of us seem to ignite very easily, Miss Hughes. (*He moves away* C)

SHIRLEY. Oooh, there speaks the managing director. I wonder what your typists say about you.

VICTOR. It really doesn't concern me, as long as the post's out on time and they can read their own shorthand.

SHIRLEY. Don't you use dictaphones?

VICTOR. No. Dictaphones don't cross their legs. (*He stops sharply, realizes his mistake, and begins to laugh*)

SHIRLEY (*rising and moving to him*) There, you see. I was right. I can tell. I can always tell. (*She hugs his arm—an impulsive, demonstrative, uninhibited sort of girl*)

(VICTOR *laughs.* JOAN *enters from the kitchen.* VICTOR *sees Joan and laughs all the more*)

VICTOR. Hello, darling—this is Shirley. (*After a pause*) Did you know about her?

JOAN. Let's say I'm not surprised.

VICTOR (*assuming that they are both talking about Giles*) Ah! You had your suspicions!

JOAN. How could you bring her here with Giles due at any moment? What will he think? Please, Victor, take her somewhere else.

(JOAN *exits to the kitchen*)

VICTOR. What's she running on about?

SHIRLEY. She thinks I'm yours.

VICTOR. Mine?

SHIRLEY (*sitting in the armchair*) Your you know what.

VICTOR. Why on earth should she think that?

SHIRLEY. Past experience, from the sound of it. Hey, is she the one who sends the cast-iron fruit cakes?

VICTOR (*absently, wondering what to do*) I don't eat cake, so I'm not really qualified to give an opinion.

SHIRLEY. I threw the last one to the birds. It's been on my conscience ever since.

VICTOR. I'd better go and explain. (*He moves to the kitchen*)

SHIRLEY. Go on, then. Ask her to forgive you for something you haven't done.

VICTOR (*stopping; needled*) What have you got against my wife, apart from her Rich Dundee?

SHIRLEY. Nothing. It's just that I hate to see a man crawl, that's all.

VICTOR. I wasn't going to crawl. I was just going to put her mind at rest.

SHIRLEY. Does she always go straight into orbit every time she finds you talking to a girl? You must have an awful lot of explaining to do.

VICTOR. I thought Giles might have written to her . . . (*He wanders behind the chaise-longue down L and back C*)

SHIRLEY. You didn't mention Giles.

VICTOR. I never got the chance, did I?

SHIRLEY. That's what I mean. It was a case of you plus girl equals dirty old man and you'll hear from my solicitors in the morning.

VICTOR. She's a bit twitched up today—because Giles is coming home.

SHIRLEY. Huh! Fancy getting twitched up about Giles!

VICTOR (*moving to Shirley*) Is there a single member of my family who meets with your approval?

SHIRLEY. Yes. You.

VICTOR. Oh, that's very flattering but . . .

(MARTIN *enters from the kitchen. He wears a jacket over his apron and looks rather like a milkman*)

MARTIN. I'm sorry to interrupt you.

VICTOR. Two pints, please.

MARTIN. Joanie was wondering if I could drop your . . .

VICTOR. Friend?

MARTIN. At the station or somewhere.

VICTOR. Really.

MARTIN (*to Victor*) Yes. May I move your car? It's blocking mine in. (*He moves down L*)

VICTOR (*moving to Martin; fuming*) No, you may not move my car

—neither may you see *my* guests off *my* premises without *my* permission.

MARTIN. Joanie's terribly upset.

VICTOR. I'm very sorry to hear it, but she's only got herself to blame.

MARTIN. Any woman would be the same.

VICTOR. Any reasonable woman would have made sure of her facts.

MARTIN. Are you suggesting that Joanie is unreasonable?

VICTOR. You make it sound like blasphemy. I think she's off her usually level head.

MARTIN. Perhaps you expect her to welcome your—er—indiscretions.

VICTOR (*moving up* C *on to the rostrum*) Please don't refer to my friend as an indiscretion. You'll hurt her feelings.

MARTIN (*following Victor*) And Joanie's feelings don't matter, I suppose.

VICTOR. You can suppose what you like. Only don't do it here.

MARTIN. What shall I tell her?

VICTOR. That's entirely up to you.

MARTIN. Is there any message?

VICTOR. I don't communicate with my wife by carrier pigeon. So fly away. Shoo! (*He waves Martin away*)

MARTIN. I hope you know what you're doing, Victor.

(MARTIN *exits to the kitchen*)

VICTOR. Exit St George with banner drooping. A knight in cashmere socks.

SHIRLEY. *Cashmere* socks?

VICTOR. Yes, he's got a sensitive skin. I'd dearly love to relieve him of it. (*He moves down* L)

SHIRLEY. Oooh, vicious! Who is he, anyway?

VICTOR. Well, he's a sort of remnant. Joan was engaged to him—when I—er—well, disengaged her, I suppose.

SHIRLEY. How?

VICTOR. Does it matter?

SHIRLEY. Oh, go on. I'm curious.

VICTOR (*sitting on the chaise-longue*) Well, a party of us went to a prom one night. I only went because Joan was going. I soon got tired of watching the conductor's arse and hoping he'd fall off his rostrum—so we nipped out between movements and we went for a walk in the park. (*Explaining*) There's a park opposite the Albert Hall, you see.

SHIRLEY (*taking a cigarette from the table* C *and lighting it*) No, really?

VICTOR. I'm sorry—I thought you came from Manchester.

SHIRLEY (*moving to Victor*) Even Mancunians can get to know London. Anyway, I was born in Harrogate.

VICTOR. I thought people only died in Harrogate.

SHIRLEY. It's not all bath chairs. It's jolly pleasant.

VICTOR. Why did you leave it, then?

SHIRLEY. To get away from home.

VICTOR. Oh, another refugee from parental injustice.

SHIRLEY (*sitting in front of the fire again*) From constant disapproval. What's he waiting for, anyway?

VICTOR. Who?

SHIRLEY. The displaced fiancé.

VICTOR (*moving* C) He's not waiting for anything. It's just got to be a habit with him. He enjoys family life without any of the responsibilities. He sits on the sidelines making mental notes of my failings and thinking what a magnificent husband and father he would have been. Ha! Imagine him raising a family! As much as he can do to raise a smile.

SHIRLEY. I think you're being vulgar.

VICTOR. You don't miss much, do you? No wonder they couldn't hold you in Harrogate. (*Moving on to the rostrum; with another bout of anger*) Is it fair? Every week-end I'm marooned up here with a gaggle of relatives whose antiquity would startle you into supporting euthanasia.

(MARTIN's *face appears at the kitchen window.* VICTOR *goes and breathes on the glass.* MARTIN *immediately disappears*)

And while I'm obliging her by being civil to them all and tolerating him, she's suspicious of me. God! It's enough to make you . . . (*He moves down* LC)

SHIRLEY. The volcano's rumbling.

VICTOR. What's that?

SHIRLEY. Giles says that living with you is like camping on the edge of a volcano.

VICTOR (*moving to Shirley*) I'll say this much for Giles. If he can cope with a girl like you, he's got more spirit than I gave him credit for.

SHIRLEY. What makes you think he can cope with me?

VICTOR. I assumed.

SHIRLEY. Never assume. Your wife has just assumed, and look where she is. Sobbing her heart out in the kitchen.

VICTOR. Oh, lord, I hope not. I was just about to put her right when Martin came bustling in full of self-importance, like a pregnant hen. Have you ever felt like that?

SHIRLEY. What, like a pregnant hen?

VICTOR. No—full of virtue and about to do the decent thing— then goaded into doing exactly the opposite.

SHIRLEY. Let's go and tell her who I am. (*She rises*)

VICTOR. You've changed your tune, haven't you?

SHIRLEY. Yes, my better nature got the better of me.

(JOAN and MARTIN *enter from the kitchen looking forbidding*)

VICTOR. Come on then—oh, too late. They're bringing up the heavy guns. Hallo? Come to show a united front?

(SHIRLEY *decides to make the first move, and goes smilingly to Joan*)

SHIRLEY. I'm really terribly sorry, I'm afraid it was my fault—
I . . .

JOAN (*moving behind the chaise-longue*) Yes, it probably was.

(SHIRLEY *looks helplessly at Victor*)

VICTOR. All right, that's it. Come on, Shirley, let's go for a
stroll round the garden, work up an appetite for lunch. (*He takes
Shirley's hand and moves to the window up* R)

JOAN. Do you expect me to give her lunch?

VICTOR. Why not? (*Jerking his thumb towards Martin*) I've been
feeding him for the last twenty years!

(VICTOR *and* SHIRLEY *exit up* R. JOAN *goes to the armchair and picks
up the crash helmet*)

JOAN. What d'you make of this?

MARTIN. She must have come on a motor-bike. (*He moves to
her*)

JOAN. Good God—he's got himself a ton-up rocker.

MARTIN. She's rather pretty—in an ordinary sort of way.

JOAN (*moving down* L *and putting the helmet on the table below the
drinks cabinet*) Imagine bringing her here and expecting me to enter-
tain her! I've always known that Victor plays around a bit, in fact
I've turned a blind eye so often I'm beginning to think I've got im-
paired vision on one side. But how can I turn a blind eye when she's
under my nose. (*She sits on the chaise-longue down stage*)

MARTIN (*sitting beside her*) Tricky. The annoying part is that you
and I have mostly tried to abide by the rules.

JOAN. Mostly, yes.

MARTIN. Despite considerable temptation.

JOAN. And ample opportunity.

MARTIN. It hasn't been easy.

JOAN. It hasn't. But still, you've had your music.

MARTIN. And you've had Victor.

JOAN. He's no business to be so attractive. If only he'd show his
age. Get fat, spread a little.

MARTIN. Do you know, Joanie—I've kept my weight steady ever
since I left the service.

JOAN. I wish he'd go bald. A nice shiny billiard-ball bald.

MARTIN. He'll probably crumble suddenly one day.

JOAN. One of his secretaries had a crush on him, did I ever tell
you?

MARTIN. Yes, you have mentioned it. (*He rises and moves to the
armchair*)

JOAN (*rising and moving to the window up* L) She used to write to me
in the most lyrical terms. The letters were meant to be consoling,
if you please. She wrote, "Anyone married to a sun-god must
expect him to warm others as well."

Martin. I hope you didn't show it to him.
Joan. I burned it at once.
Martin (*sitting in the armchair*) Good.
Joan. He's quite conceited enough as it is. Look at him warming her with his ultra-violet smile.

(Martin *rises and moves to the window up* R)

It's time he went into an eclipse.
Martin. They're coming back.
Joan (*moving to the chaise-longue*) I shall ignore them. (*She sits*)

(Martin *sits in the armchair. They both stare ahead, with stony faces.* Victor *enters up* R *with* Shirley)

Victor (*mildly*) I think it's coming on to rain. Never mind, do the plants good. Into each life a little rain must fall. Isn't that a beautiful thought? Hands up all those who think it's beautiful. (*After a pause*) Pity old George isn't here. He could have told us what happened to him in Oslo.

(Shirley *moves below Martin and sits in front of the fire*)

You know, when I was a little boy I had a hamster. What made me think of that? There's a reason for everything, you know. Now what made me think of my hamster? (*He peers into Martin's face*) No, you're not like a hamster, Martin. At least, not from the front. A dear little chap he was. They're members of the rat family, you know—(*looking at Joan*)—but we all have relations we're not proud of. He had a soft sniffly nose and eyes like blobs of black ink. He used to sit on my hand throbbing away. Ah, now I know what made me think of him. (*He squats beside Shirley*) I'm feeling unloved at this particular moment, and Hammy loved me without question. I think I might buy another hamster. In fact I might go in for animals in a big way. I'd rather like to start a private zoo.
Shirley. I'll love you if you like.
Victor. Would you really?
Shirley. I'd be cheaper to keep than polar bears.
Victor (*rising to the fireplace*) Ah, but you couldn't grow your own fur coat.

(Giles *enters up* L, *wearing a windcheater and polo neck sweater and carrying a rucksack to which is attached a crash helmet. He is nineteen. He looks hot, and wipes the sweat and rain from his forehead with a black-oiled hand*)

Giles. Hullo, Mum.
Joan. Giles!
Giles (*to Shirley, putting his rucksack down* L *of the armchair*) Oh, you got here then.
Shirley. What does it look like?
Giles. Met the folks, have you? Good. Hullo, Uncle Martin.

(*He half glances at Victor and mutters*) 'llo, Dad. What's for lunch? I'm starving.

(GILES *exits to the kitchen.* VICTOR *moves above the armchair and, using his hands like antlers, makes signs at Joan*)

(*Off*) Anything worth noshing in here? I'm starving.

SHIRLEY (*rising*) Isn't that typical of you! The first thing you think of.

(*As the two young people quarrel,* JOAN *and* MARTIN *realize their mistake.* GILES *enters with a bottle of lager. He helps himself to a bowl of crisps on the drinks cabinet, and stands behind the chaise-longue, down stage*)

GILES (*as he enters*) It'll make a welcome change from your usual offerings—pre-packed, pre-cooked, just heat and serve up. Just eat and throw up.

SHIRLEY. I do my best. I finish later than you and I've got farther to travel, but there's always a meal on the table before your key's even in the door.

GILES. I don't know how you manage it!

SHIRLEY. I shift, that's how. And what do you do? Apart from criticizing my cooking?

GILES. I eat it.

(JOAN *gives Victor a long, hard look.* VICTOR *smiles and bows*)

JOAN. Giles, why on earth didn't you tell me you were bringing a friend?

GILES. She didn't decide to come until the last minute.

SHIRLEY. You didn't want me to come.

GILES. You were the one who didn't want to come.

SHIRLEY. I only said I didn't want to because I knew you didn't really want me to.

GILES. I did want you to. But I said I didn't because I knew you didn't really want to.

SHIRLEY. Well, I did.

GILES. What?

SHIRLEY. Want to come.

GILES. So I brought you, didn't I?

SHIRLEY. Yes.

GILES. So that's all right, then.

SHIRLEY. It's all right with me.

GILES. It's all right, with me, too.

SHIRLEY (*doubtfully*) But I don't know if it's all right with your mother.

JOAN (*who has been looking from one to the other like a spectator at a tennis match*) It would have been all righter—better—if you'd arrived together.

GILES. Elsie kept stopping.

JOAN. How many girls have you brought?

GILES. The bike's called Elsie. Shirley went ahead in a milk wagon.

JOAN (*to Shirley*) Why didn't you say so?

SHIRLEY. I did try.

JOAN (*nonplussed, but only for a moment*) It's all Victor's fault.

VICTOR. I was waiting for this squabble to reach its inevitable conclusion.

SHIRLEY. Giles.

GILES. What?

SHIRLEY. Introduce me properly.

GILES. What d'you want? A fanfare?

SHIRLEY. You've got disgusting manners.

GILES. I've been pushing Elsie and revving her up for three sweating miles. I'm not feeling exactly courtly. However—Shirley Hughes—Father, Mother, Martin Morley. Sort yourselves out.

SHIRLEY (*moving to Martin*) How do you do. (*She shakes hands*)

MARTIN. How do you do.

SHIRLEY (*going to Victor*) How do you do. (*She shakes hands*)

VICTOR. How do you do. (*He pretends to curtsy*)

SHIRLEY (*moving to Joan*) How do you do. (*She shakes hands*)

JOAN. We had no idea. Giles writes letters like telegrams.

SHIRLEY. Dear Mum, I'm okay, thanks for the grub, love and kisses.

JOAN. Oh, you read them.

SHIRLEY. He wouldn't write at all, if I didn't make him. I knew you'd be anxious.

JOAN (*with difficulty*) That was sweet of you.

SHIRLEY. I may have a son of my own one day.

GILES. Don't overdo it, love.

SHIRLEY. Drop dead.

JOAN. Tell me, dear, how did you meet each other?

SHIRLEY. We met over the cheese.

JOAN. In a restaurant?

SHIRLEY. No, in a supermarket.

VICTOR. You were buying cheese?

SHIRLEY. I was buying cheese. Giles was selling it.

VICTOR. Selling cheese!

JOAN. That's what I thought she said.

VICTOR. Selling cheese?

JOAN. Victor!

MARTIN (*pouring oil*) Cheese is a wholesome dairy product. Rich in protein and calcium.

VICTOR (*niggled*) I don't deny it. I'm very fond of cheese. In fact I'm addicted to the stuff. But I wouldn't devote my life to it!

JOAN. You promised.

(VICTOR *subsides a little*)

GILES. I haven't devoted my life to it. People should try all sorts of jobs before they settle down. Not to be slotted into their father's factory as though it had been predestined. I happen to be happier with cheese than I was with cadmium-plated components.

SHIRLEY (*laughing*) Actually he got rather good with the patter. "Take the old man a pound of Wensleydale. Or a chunk of stinking Stilton, that'll put hairs on his chest." (*She looks round and becomes aware of an "atmosphere"*) Shall I go on?

GILES. I wouldn't dream of trying to stop you.

SHIRLEY. Well, the manager was choking him off because he dropped a piece of cheese on the floor, blew on it and put it back on the scales.

JOAN. Oh, Giles!

GILES. It was a clean floor.

SHIRLEY. "Didn't they teach you elementary 'ygiene at Eton and 'Arrow?" Horrible man. So I stuck up for Giles. "It doesn't matter," I said. "He can blow on my bit of Cheshire any time." And that's how it started.

(*There is a silence*)

MARTIN. D'you know—that's rather a lovely story.

VICTOR. Very moving.

GILES. I've got a better job now. With rising prospects.

JOAN. That's good.

GILES. And every chance of reaching the top.

JOAN (*to Victor*) There you are.

SHIRLEY. Window cleaning.

VICTOR (*moving to the stool*) Next week lavatory attendant. Every chance of reaching the bottom. (*He half sits, realizes what he has said, finally sits on the stool*)

GILES (*after a slight pause*) I'm self-employed. Got my own ladder and shammy leather.

SHIRLEY. Mrs Kershaw says you smear the corners.

GILES (*blowing a swift raspberry*) —to Mrs Kershaw.

SHIRLEY. Isn't he uncouth?

GILES (*rising*) I'm filthy. (*He looks at his hands*)

SHIRLEY. There's no need to boast about it.

GILES. I meant literally.

SHIRLEY. So did I.

GILES (*picking up his rucksack*) I must go up and wash.

SHIRLEY. Yes, I could do with a scrub myself.

JOAN. Of course. Show Shirley where everything is.

GILES. She knows her way around all right. (*He puts his arm round Shirley and squeezes her*)

JOAN (*faintly*) I meant the clean towels.

GILES (*putting his hand on the nape of Shirley's neck*) Come on then, passion flower. (*He propels her down L*)

SHIRLEY (*suddenly with a broad Lancashire accent*) Get yer filthy mucky 'and off me clean neck, yob.

GILES. She's crazy about me.

(GILES *and* SHIRLEY *exit down* L. JOAN, *dying to speak to Victor alone, gestures to Martin to go into the kitchen*)

JOAN. Put the beans on, Martin.
MARTIN. Hm?
JOAN. The beans!
MARTIN (*moving to the kitchen door*) Oh yes, of course. Salt?
VICTOR. Just a pinch, dear.

(MARTIN *exits to the kitchen*)

I suppose you want to offer me a tiny apology.
JOAN. I think it's the boot on the other foot. You made no attempt to explain who she was.
VICTOR. You went straight into orbit, before I could even open my mouth.
JOAN. You left me under a misapprehension.
VICTOR. Misappre-nothing. You were enjoying your home-made melodrama. Pity to spoil it.
JOAN. It wouldn't be the first time we've had a misunderstanding over a girl.
VICTOR. I'll ignore that. I'll have five hundred lines on my desk, first thing Monday morning. "I must not accuse my husband of infidelity on flimsy evidence."
JOAN. I wouldn't call her flimsy . . .
VICTOR (*picking up Shirley's things from the armchair and throwing them over the chair up* R) She's certainly not hefty. (*He sits in the armchair*)
JOAN. It was silly of me, now I come to think of it.
VICTOR. I glad you realize that, darling.
JOAN (*rising and moving* C) A young girl like that. I mean, let's face it, she can't be more than eighteen-nineteen.
VICTOR. So?
JOAN. Well, let's face it.
VICTOR. Let's face what?
JOAN. Well, darling, you are getting a bit—you know . . .
VICTOR. No, I don't know.
JOAN. I don't want to have to spell it out.
VICTOR. I'd rather you did.
JOAN. All right, then. A bit long in the tooth.
VICTOR. Thank you very much.
JOAN. You're not going to sulk, I hope.
VICTOR. What d'you expect me to do? A handstand or some-thing?
JOAN (*sitting on the* L *arm of the armchair*) We're none of us getting any younger.
VICTOR. You speak for yourself.
JOAN. When you see each other every day you hardly notice the changes. (*She points to his chin and forehead*) A slackening here, a couple of lines there. But I adore you and I always will. Even when you're completely and utterly ga-ga. I haven't hurt you, have I?

VICTOR. No, no, I love it. Let's have some more.

JOAN. I'm sorry, darling, but you're always saying that *tempus fugits.*

VICTOR. It's different when I say it. I can say it. But you can't.

JOAN. It's for your own good.

(VICTOR *stands in front of the fire*)

I don't want you to make a fool of yourself. (*After a short pause*) Again.

VICTOR. Again?

JOAN. I was thinking of Valerie.

VICTOR. You've got a bloody long memory.

JOAN (*changing the subject*) Odd that Giles never mentioned Shirley. They seem to be fairly intimate.

VICTOR. Intimate—I think they're living together.

JOAN (*rising*) Surely not. He would have written.

VICTOR. Yes. "Dear Mum. Cake arrived intact. Am shacked up with Shirley. Love Giles."

JOAN. I don't like it.

VICTOR. He's the one who likes it. I only wish he had as much success with his career.

JOAN. You'll have to give him some advice, Victor.

VICTOR. I thought he might give me some.

JOAN. Encourage him to discuss his problems.

VICTOR (*moving to the table* C *and lighting a cigarette*) I don't think he's got any problems.

JOAN. What sort of father are you? You should be his guide and friend.

VICTOR. Every suggestion I make falls on stony ground. Perhaps I'll try a different approach.

JOAN. What?

VICTOR. *Laissez-faire.*

JOAN. No, I think we really must say something to him.

(GILES *enters*)

GILES. Shirley's still doing her face. (*He takes an apple from the bowl, sits on the back of the chaise-longue and begins noisily eating*)

VICTOR. I see.

(JOAN *tries twice to begin a sentence but gives up*)

VICTOR (*after a lengthy silence, to Joan*) Where's Martin with his polyfilla? (*He sits on the chaise-longue*)

JOAN. He doesn't want to intrude on a family conference.

VICTOR. Do you call this a conference? All I can hear is a medley of chewing, crunching and *champing.*

(GILES *stops eating, the apple half-way to his lips.* VICTOR *and* GILES *glare at each other*)

JOAN. Finish, Giles. But hurry.

(GILES *returns to demolishing the apple with great determination*)

VICTOR. He's doing it on purpose.

GILES. I'm only eating an apple.

VICTOR (*picking up a piece*) You dropped a bit.

GILES. Is it against the law?

JOAN. He is only eating an apple.

(VICTOR *shrugs helplessly.* SHIRLEY *enters and moves* RC, *patting Giles on the shoulder as she passes him*)

SHIRLEY. Hello, gutsy.

(*For answer,* GILES *throws the core at her, but* SHIRLEY *ducks and the apple rebounds off the fireplace in bits*)

JOAN. Giles, do be careful.

GILES (*moving down* R *and retrieving the bits*) Sorry, Mum, sorry. I thought I was at home.

JOAN (*pained*) You are at home.

(MARTIN *enters from the kitchen*)

MARTIN. Everything's under control.

JOAN (*moving to Victor then to the kitchen door*) Perhaps we'd better go in for lunch.

VICTOR (*rising*) I think we'd better, before there's bloodshed. (*He takes Shirley's arm*) Come along, Shirley—you can sit next to me.

SHIRLEY. Oh super—I'm absolutely ravenous.

VICTOR (*eyeing Shirley*) I'm a bit hungry myself.

(SHIRLEY *and* VICTOR *exit down* L)

GILES (*crossing down* L) Well, get Dad playing the host!

(GILES *exits down* L)

JOAN (*moving up* L) Yes, let's hope that's all he's playing at.

JOAN *exits to the kitchen.* MARTIN *begins to follow her, but is caught by the kitchen door rebounding in his face, as—*

the CURTAIN *falls*

ACT II

SCENE—*The same. Late evening, the same day.*

The three oil lamps hanging on the wall are lit, and also the table lamp on the drinks cabinet. The door down L *is open.*

When the CURTAIN *rises,* VICTOR *is discovered sitting in the armchair with his feet on the stool, smoking.* JOAN *is sitting on the chaise-longue. They are both watching television, which is in the corner down* R. JOAN *rises, moves down* L *and listens at the door.*

VICTOR. What's the matter?

JOAN. I thought I heard Giles coming down.

VICTOR. Evidently he doesn't want to be cross-examined.

JOAN (*moving to Victor*) I thought we might have a nice cosy chat.

VICTOR. Must we?

JOAN (*switching off the television and pushing the set against the wall down* R) Well, don't you want to know more?

VICTOR. I'd rather watch TV.

JOAN. You don't seem to care. I asked Martin to take Shirley for a walk after supper so that we could get Giles on his own . . .

VICTOR. And grill him.

JOAN (*moving down* L) Yes. *No.* (*She listens again*) I think he's locked himself in the loo.

VICTOR. He used to do that when he was a small boy in trouble, remember?

JOAN. Yes, and the bathroom. He'd turn all the taps full on. (*She wanders up* C)

VICTOR. Curious how he always turns to plumbing for comfort.

JOAN. Those are the only two rooms which bolt from the inside. Oh, my head aches. Don't they fight, those two!

VICTOR. She's a match for him, though. I love their wide range of epithets. The last one I caught was rotten, blue-nosed baboon.

JOAN. Is that what she called him?

VICTOR. No, that's what he called her. Giles leans towards the zoological. Shirley goes in for straightforward simple abuse.

JOAN. I don't understand it.

VICTOR. It's the new, trendy, swinging sixties love-talk. I hate you, you squint-eyed, knock-kneed moron. Kiss me.

JOAN. If you spoke to me like that I'd burst into tears.

VICTOR. You have to be tough and resilient these days. It also helps to be stone-deaf.

JOAN. How are you and Giles getting on?

VICTOR. There's an uneasy truce.

JOAN. Are you going to offer him his old job back? (*She sits on the chaise-longue*)

VICTOR. What, after he threw it in my face?

JOAN. You can't just leave him to drift.

VICTOR. If he's bent on self-destruction, there's precious little I can do about it. Oh, well, at least he's still got the old-fashioned idea of working for a living. Do you know what I think he should do?

(GILES *enters down* L *and wanders above the armchair*)

GILES. Are you talking about me?

VICTOR ⎫
JOAN ⎭ (*together*) No.

GILES. Shirley not back yet?

JOAN. They may have popped into the *King Charles*. I say won't the regulars stare!

VICTOR. They'll wonder what Martin's up to—out with a dolly bird.

GILES (*carelessly*) She's not bad, is she?

VICTOR. She's not bad at all.

(VICTOR *and* JOAN *exchange looks.* GILES *takes the stool from under Victor's feet and sits in front of the fireplace*)

JOAN. We don't know very much about her.

GILES (*quick to anger, like his father*) Why don't you ask me who her people are? That's what you're driving at, isn't it? Who are they? What are they? And are they our sort?

VICTOR. Now don't be rude to your mother, Giles. She worries herself to death over you, sends you fruit cakes—and things . . .

JOAN. I was only trying to get an overall picture. Are you engaged?

GILES: Engaged in what.

VICTOR. Affianced.

GILES. Look, nobody gets engaged any more except for horsey debs. It's out.

JOAN. I see. Well, if I'd known you were bringing a girl with you I wouldn't have invited Martin.

GILES. What difference does it make?

JOAN. He's got the other room.

GILES (*stubbornly*) No comprendo.

JOAN. You'll have to sleep on this. (*She indicates the chaise-longue*)

GILES. Do me a favour. My feet hang over the end.

JOAN. Not if you bend your knees. You'll have to let Shirley have your room.

GILES. Yes, she can have my room.

JOAN. Oh, good.

GILES. And I'll share it with her.

JOAN. Don't be silly, darling.

GILES. What d'you think we are? Just good friends?

JOAN (*almost in desperation*) Victor. Say something.

VICTOR (*after a pause*) Tally-ho.

GILES. Look, you wanted the overall picture. We've got this little place in Manchester. Brook Lane. Fallowfield.

VICTOR. We thought that sounded pleasantly rural, didn't we, Joan?

GILES. Oh, it's all built up now.

VICTOR. That's a pity!

GILES. Yes, streets of houses where once there were meadows.

VICTOR. Toward the latter end of the nineteenth century, I suppose.

JOAN (*moving* L *of the armchair*) When you two have finished discussing the spread of Industrial England, I've got this to say. I've never kept a disorderly house and I've no intention of starting now.

GILES. There you are, you see. As soon as I get here you start to interfere.

JOAN. But how can we possibly stand by . . .

GILES. Nobody's asking you to stand by. We're not selling tickets. Just go to bed and leave us alone. You sleep together, don't you, on the strength of some archaic ceremony you went through in the year dot.

VICTOR. He's got a point there, you know.

JOAN. Whose side are you on?

VICTOR. You told me to try to see his point of view.

JOAN. That's before I knew what it was. How can we possibly allow a young girl to—I'd feel responsible. She might be my own daughter.

GILES. But she isn't, is she?

JOAN (*moving* LC) She's somebody's daughter. Though what sort of parents she can have who let her run wild . . .

GILES. She's not running wild. She's living with me. I'm all right, aren't I? A clean-limbed, true-blue pukka type. I'm your sort.

JOAN. But you're not married.

GILES. Not yet—but we might go through the formalities one day, if we get the urge.

VICTOR. You seem to be putting the urge before the formalities.

GILES. We've got to see whether it works out.

VICTOR. It can't work out, can it? Nobody's going to make the effort to keep a contract that hasn't been signed. You're putting the cart before the horse. In other words, the whole arrangement's a non-starter.

GILES. When two people decide to shack up together——

(JOAN *looks pained.* VICTOR *moves above the chaise-longue to the drinks and pours two brandies*)

—it's between them. Not between their parents, cousins, aunts, Uncle Tom Cobblers and all. Basically, it's nothing but jealousy. That's what's at the bottom of all this disapproval. Because the last generation were so frustrated, they can't bear to see us getting any fun out of it.

JOAN. I've never seen two people getting less fun in my life. You do nothing but snarl at each other.

GILES. We bite each other, too, but that doesn't mean to say we're not in love. Smarming is out.

VICTOR (*moving to Joan; amused*) D'you hear that, Joanie? Smarming's out, biting's in. (*He hands Joan her drink*) Here, you'd better drink this. I'm really very grateful to you, Giles. You're putting us through an intensive course in modern habits and customs. (*To Joan*) I hadn't realized how out of touch we were, darling. I think we ought to get a divorce and live in sin.

GILES (*laughing*) Sin. Sin. What a funny old word. That's really quaint.

VICTOR (*slightly piqued*) What's the new word for it?

GILES. There isn't one. The whole concept of sin is out. Fini. Kaput.

VICTOR (*taking a pad and pencil from the writing desk*) I must make a note of that. Sin is out, is it? Fini. Kaput.

JOAN. Don't encourage him.

VICTOR (*moving above the table* C) Well, you told me to try to see his point of view.

JOAN. I didn't ask you to support it.

VICTOR. Oh, I see—you wanted me to find out what it was and then condemn it?

JOAN. Please be serious. *Laisser-faire's* all very well, but there's a limit to what you can *laisser* him *faire* here.

VICTOR (*putting his pad and pencil on the table* C) Now listen, Giles. (*He sits in the armchair*) Quite seriously, we didn't come up to Manchester to check on you, we respected your right to live your own life—but whilst you're in our house I think you should respect the conventions we live by, whether you believe in them or not . . .

JOAN. And sleep on the chaise-longue.

VICTOR. Yes.

GILES (*rising*) I'd almost forgotten how pompous you can be.

VICTOR (*rising*) I haven't forgotten how insolent you can be.

JOAN (*rising*) Can't we settle this peacefully?

GILES (*moving* L *of Victor*) I didn't want to come here in the first place, and I'm not staying. We'll find somewhere in the village, or we'll take the late train to London.

VICTOR. You'll stay here and you'll bloody well behave yourself.

GILES. I'll stay here if we can have the bedroom. Otherwise not.

(GILES *exits down* L)

JOAN. This is blackmail.

VICTOR (*after a pause*) Yes.

JOAN. How I'd love to smack him!

VICTOR (*sitting in the armchair*) He's just showing off, darling.

JOAN (*crossing to Victor*) You'll have to be firm.

VICTOR. You realize we're in a cleft stick. If I insist, you might not see him again for another six months, or six years for that matter. I'm not risking your reproaches again. You can decide this time.

JOAN. I need another drink. (*She goes to the drinks and pours herself another brandy*)

(MARTIN *enters up* L *and stands aside.* SHIRLEY *enters,* MARTIN *draws the curtains*)

MARTIN. Hello, we're back. I showed Shirley the old Cross and the stocks and then we had a quick drink in the *King Charles.*

(SHIRLEY *moves down* L *of the armchair*)

VICTOR. It gets very crowded in there on a Saturday night.

MARTIN. Yes, somebody was pounding the piano as though they had a grudge against it.

JOAN. You will have loved that!

MARTIN. It was a relief to get out into the cool night air. Lovely moon tonight.

SHIRLEY. I didn't want to stay anyway. I'm so tired. I'm absolutely exhausted. (*She sinks down by Victor, resting her head on his knee*)

JOAN. I suppose you left Manchester very early this morning.

SHIRLEY. Seven o'clock. Seven o' flipping clock. (*She yawns*)

VICTOR. Ah—(*he is about to put his arm round her, then thinks better of it and just pats her*)—it's been a long day for you.

(GILES *enters* L *from the kitchen, smoking a cigarette, crosses and sits on the stool down* R)

GILES (*as he moves*) Oh, you're back. Good. Ready for bed?

SHIRLEY. No.

JOAN. That was a straight answer.

MARTIN. Shirley's a very direct sort of person.

SHIRLEY. I hope I haven't offended you.

MARTIN (*moving* C) No, no, not at all. As a matter of fact, I found our conversation most—stimulating.

GILES. I'm sure.

SHIRLEY. You weren't there.

GILES. I don't have to be.

SHIRLEY. Martin meant it was mentally stimulating.

MARTIN. Yes, of course I did. As a matter of fact we were talking about music. Amongst other things.

SHIRLEY. Like how it can affect your mood.

MARTIN (*to Joan*) The way a brass band makes everybody want to wave their flag.

SHIRLEY. We were talking about smootchy type music.

GILES. I bet you were.

SHIRLEY. Smootchy music turns me on. (*She plays seductively with Victor's leg*)

VICTOR (*shifts uneasily*) Yes, I like a good tune.

SHIRLEY. You know, Martin's so clever. He told me all sorts of exciting things.

JOAN. I'm glad you got on so well.

MARTIN. Just being friendly.

SHIRLEY. Well, there's no point in conversation if you don't get to know each other. People are so exciting when you dig beneath the surface.

(GILES *stubs out his cigarette in the ashtray in the fireplace*)

VICTOR. You believe in getting down to essentials, do you?

SHIRLEY. One learns the most surprising things.

MARTIN. Yes.

GILES (*to Martin*) Did she ask if you were a virgin?

JOAN (*shocked*) I hope not.

GILES. That's the first thing she asked me.

SHIRLEY. And you told me a lie.

(GILES *turns away.* VICTOR *is amused*)

GILES (*recovering*) Did she, Uncle Martin?

(MARTIN *laughs self-consciously and makes hurriedly for the door down* L)

MARTIN. Well, it's—er—been a lovely evening. I think I'll turn in. The Sabbath will find me fresh and bright. Good night, everybody.

(MARTIN *exits down* L)

VICTOR. He looked a little flushed around the gills.

GILES (*moving* C) Well, I think I'll turn in. (*He looks at his mother— it's a challenge*) Are you coming to bed now, Shirley?

JOAN (*moving to Giles*) Now, Giles, I've told you before, it's— it's——

(JOAN *and* GILES *glare at each other*)

—not a full-sized double bed. (*Finally*) I hope you children will be comfortable. (*She moves to the end of the drinks cabinet*)

VICTOR. It's three foot nine, actually. That gives you twenty-two and a half inches each.

(SHIRLEY *moves to the upstage end of the fireplace*)

(*To Shirley*) Would you like to borrow the ironing board?

SHIRLEY. No, thank you. I've got sharp elbows. (*She makes a nudging movement to prove her point*)

JOAN (*moving down* L) I'm going to take one of my sleeping pills. The Sabbath will find me doped and sluggish, but at least I shall be unconscious for seven blessed hours. Are you coming, Victor?

VICTOR. I think I'll read for a while, darling.

JOAN. Don't sit up too late with your horror stories.

VICTOR. They're science fiction.

JOAN. What's the difference? If there's any truth in them, the future will be sheer horror anyway. Already things aren't what they used to be. Good night.

(*Everybody answers.* JOAN *exits down* L)

SHIRLEY. She makes me feel like the Whore of Babylon.

GILES. She'll adjust to the situation.

VICTOR. I bought some books this morning. I wonder where I left them? (*Moving up* L) In the car, that's where they are. Yes, they're in the car—do excuse me.

(VICTOR *exits to the kitchen*)

GILES (*relaxing at once in the armchair*) I can't relax when he's around. You can never forget he's there. He fills the whole room with his ego. Me, me, me.

SHIRLEY (*takes a cigarette from the table* C *and picks up the lighter*) He's got a strong personality.

GILES. He's too much.

SHIRLEY. You're jealous because he's mature and successful.

GILES. He's jealous because I'm young and free.

SHIRLEY (*wandering up* C) What did they say while I was out? Any objections to us sleeping together?

GILES (*untruthfully*) Oh, good lord, no.

SHIRLEY (*lighting her cigarette*) Wasn't your mother shocked?

GILES. She soon capitulated.

SHIRLEY. What?

GILES. Adjusted.

SHIRLEY. You are lucky having such broadminded parents. Mine went clean up the wall because I was caught necking in a car.

GILES. Whose car?

SHIRLEY (*replacing the lighter*) The car of the bloke I was necking with, of course. (*She sits on the chaise-longue*) We were parked outside the front gate and that should have proved how innocent we were, I mean we could have easily gone down a dark lane.

GILES. I suppose you've got to think of the neighbours when you live at the vicarage.

SHIRLEY. Yes, everybody took a fierce interest in my comings and goings. I couldn't move an inch.

GILES. Poor girl, she was only the vicar's daughter—but she played a lot of hymns.

SHIRLEY. I think I'll sleep down here.

GILES. You can't possibly.

SHIRLEY. After five hours on Elsie I could sleep on a clothes line.

GILES. But how will it look?

SHIRLEY. Respectable.

GILES (*moving to Shirley*) Since when have you had a narrow *petit bourgeois* outlook?

SHIRLEY. Since I've been made to feel like a tart.

GILES (*sitting on the chaise-longue*) But haven't I offered to make it legal every Saturday since Easter? The licence is rapidly running out.

SHIRLEY. The thing is we *don't* any more. We haven't for the last three weeks.

GILES. Whose fault is that?

SHIRLEY. Soon we'll have to decide whether we are going to stay together or split up. Anyway, this is quite comfortable. (*She pushes Giles off, and lies back*) Yes, it's lovely.

GILES (*moving away* C) I went to a lot of trouble to get that bedroom.

SHIRLEY. Ooooooh, and you said . . .

GILES. You'll make me look such a fool.

SHIRLEY. You don't need any help.

GILES. Only for one night. (*He moves to Shirley*)

SHIRLEY. What is this? "Be king to sex maniacs week"?

GILES (*squatting by her*) Just for one night.

SHIRLEY. If you promise not to try anything.

GILES. Why? Have you gone off it?

SHIRLEY. No, but I've gone off you. I prefer someone more mature like your father—I really don't know how a divine creature like that sired a slob like you.

GILES. Didn't anyone ever tell you?

SHIRLEY (*rising*) Spare me your schoolboy innuendoes, dear. And don't forget. It's back to back.

(VICTOR *appears at the kitchen door and stands watching*)

GILES (*rising*) Or how to make both ends meet.

SHIRLEY (*moving down* L) Your wit paralyzes me. And watch it, mate, or . . . (*She makes nudging gestures with her elbows*)

(SHIRLEY *exits down* L. GILES *takes a drink of whisky from the bottle before following her. As he exits, he is almost choked by the whisky.* VICTOR *enters with a book, a glass of milk and a three-decker sandwich. He absent-mindedly walks along the rostrum with one foot on and the other off, stops, puts the plate and sandwich down by the armchair, switches on the standard lamp, sits in the armchair with his feet on the stool and begins to read. The lights fade to* BLACK-OUT.

When the lights come up again, VICTOR *is still reading, but his glass is empty and so is the plate.* SHIRLEY *enters down* L, *carrying a pillow and blanket*)

SHIRLEY (*genuinely surprised*) Oh. Hallo.

VICTOR (*equally so*) Oh. What time is it?

SHIRLEY. I don't know.

VICTOR (*looking at his watch*) It's ten past one. (*He rises*)

SHIRLEY. I didn't think anybody would still be up.

VICTOR. I usually sleep late on Sunday mornings—it halves the dreariest day of the week.

SHIRLEY (*putting her bedding on the chaise-longue and crossing to him*) Is that a good book?

VICTOR. Certainly not. I don't read good books. Only rubbish. This is a choice bit of rubbish about the year two thousand and seventy. We're going to be reduced to one inch in size to solve the world food problem.

SHIRLEY. That's rather a good idea. I mean, I wouldn't mind being tichy as long as everybody else was tichy too.

VICTOR. Ah, but the insects don't join in the plan——

SHIRLEY. Oh.

VICTOR. —and so they become fearsome enemies.

SHIRLEY (*moving* L) Isn't it marvellous! Fast as you solve one problem you meet up with another. (*She looks at the chaise-longue*)

VICTOR. Yes. Why did you abandon your nice warm twenty-two and a half inches?

SHIRLEY. It was getting crowded. Does the head let down?

VICTOR (*rising and moving to the chaise-longue*) Yes, I'll do it for you. There's a little catch at the back. (*He catches his finger*) Ouch! It's done that before. Rotten swine. (*He kicks it*) Tit for tat. Touch of the old Hammurabis.

SHIRLEY. Hammuwhat?

VICTOR. King Hammurabi. Ancient law-maker. An eye for an eye and a tooth for a tooth and so on. Excellent maxim, you know. Never been bettered.

(SHIRLEY *makes up the bed*)

SHIRLEY. My father turns the other cheek. He has to. It's his profession.

VICTOR. What is he, a dentist?

SHIRLEY (*laughing*) No.

VICTOR. Barber?

SHIRLEY. No.

VICTOR. I give up. (*He pauses, but as she offers no explanation, he goes to the armchair and picks up the empty plate*) Would you like a triple-decker ham, *paté*, lettuce, pickle, Worcester sauce sandwich? *Specialité de la maison?*

SHIRLEY (*looking at the empty plate*) Where is it?

VICTOR. I've eaten it. I'll get one for you, though. (*He moves towards the kitchen*)

SHIRLEY. No, thank you.

VICTOR. Throw it together in seconds.

SHIRLEY. I'm not hungry. (*She lies down on the chaise-longue*)

VICTOR. I'd better leave you, then. (*He switches off the standard lamp, then the main lights, then moves to the door down* L, *putting the plate on the drinks cabinet*)

SHIRLEY. My feet are cold.

VICTOR. You'd better cover them up, hadn't you?

SHIRLEY. Aren't you going to tuck me in?

VICTOR. I think I've forgotten how. (*He looks up the stairs to make sure no-one is coming, then tucks the blanket round her*) How's that?

SHIRLEY. Lovely. (*She puts her arms round his neck and holds him prisoner*) When are you going to kiss me?

VICTOR. I'm weighing up the pros and cons.

SHIRLEY. What's happened to your impetuosity?

VICTOR. I try to stifle it.

SHIRLEY. That's very unhealthy. (*She holds on and waits*)

VICTOR. You're so right. (*He kisses her. Whilst doing so, he puts one hand firmly behind his back*) That was much healthier, wasn't it?

SHIRLEY (*faintly*) Don't ask questions.

VICTOR. Sorry. (*He pulls away and moves to the door down* L)

SHIRLEY. What's the matter?

VICTOR. Got to stop.

SHIRLEY. Why?

VICTOR. Wife, child, home, morals, conventions, and some idiot might come down for a glass of milk.

SHIRLEY. They could go the other way.

VICTOR. No, they never do. (*Moving* C) Besides, they'd see the light.

SHIRLEY (*switching off the lamp*) What light?

VICTOR (*in the blackness*) Shirley . . .

SHIRLEY. Over here.

VICTOR. Oh! I've bumped my shin. Shirley, I've bumped my shin.

SHIRLEY. You're getting warmer.

VICTOR. You're so right. (*He switches on the main lights and the table lamp*)

(SHIRLEY *is revealed looking rather abandoned*)

SHIRLEY. What did you do that for?

VICTOR (*moving* C) I couldn't see what I was doing.

SHIRLEY. You're a coward.

VICTOR. It's not a question of cowardice. It's discretion.

SHIRLEY. Do you deny you smiled at me when I walked in?

VICTOR. I smile at hundreds of girls. Good lord, if I followed every smile to what you suggest would be the logical conclusion, I wouldn't last a week.

SHIRLEY. It wasn't an ordinary smile.

VICTOR. Yes, it was. It was my ordinary, everyday, wash-and-wear, mind-the-step, how's-the-wife smile. I flash it all over the place—(*putting the milk glass on the table* C)—and people think "what a charming fellow". It's only my close associates who know what a damned misery I am really.

SHIRLEY. You need some different close associates.

VICTOR (*moving* R) Yes, I know.

SHIRLEY. Stop moving around and come and sit down.

VICTOR. I need the exercise.

SHIRLEY. How long have you been married?

VICTOR. Longer than you've been around.

SHIRLEY. That's too long.

VICTOR. D'you think so?

SHIRLEY. There can't be many surprises left.

VICTOR. No.

SHIRLEY. You must practically know what your wife is going to say before she even says it.

VICTOR. Practically.

SHIRLEY. And she probably knows exactly what you're thinking.

VICTOR. I hope not.

SHIRLEY. I don't know how you stand it.

VICTOR. I'm out of the house a good deal, lurking in the bushes.

SHIRLEY. Naturally.

VICTOR. And I work very hard.

SHIRLEY. Ah, you escape through work. That's bad. It becomes a habit, and you forget how to relax.

VICTOR. Have you made a study of all this?

SHIRLEY. My employers usually confide in me.

VICTOR (*moving to Shirley*) How many employers have you had? I mean, how many jobs have you had?

SHIRLEY. It's always the same job. An office agency sends me out to fill short-term vacancies. I'm a temp.

VICTOR. A sort of relief typist?

SHIRLEY. Mm.

VICTOR. Don't you find it unsettling?

SHIRLEY. I don't like staying in one place too long. I always get involved in some way.

VICTOR. I can well believe it.

SHIRLEY. Come and sit down. I won't bite you.

(VICTOR, *unsure, moves above the chaise-longue and leans against the drinks cabinet*)

I wonder whether you realize nearly half your life is over.

VICTOR. More than half.

SHIRLEY. You should plan for a hundred years.

VICTOR. I'm not so optimistic.

SHIRLEY. You'd look jolly silly planning for eighty years if you suddenly found yourself stuck with an extra twenty you hadn't bargained for.

VICTOR (*sitting on the back of the chaise-longue*) That's true, very true.

SHIRLEY. So you're standing at the half-way mark, facing two roads. One's flat and smooth and easy to follow, but leads inexorably downhill . . .

VICTOR. Have you been reading *The Pilgrim's Progress?*

SHIRLEY. I used to take a Sunday School class.

VICTOR. You've lived, haven't you?

SHIRLEY. The other's steep and twisting——

VICTOR. —and leads inexorably over the edge. (*He kisses her*)

SHIRLEY. Wouldn't you rather leap over a cliff than roll into a rut?

VICTOR. Don't ask such damn silly questions. (*He kisses her again then pulls away*) Got to stop.

SHIRLEY (*annoyed again*) Why?

VICTOR (*moving* C) There's no future in this.

SHIRLEY. Who cares about the future?

VICTOR. You've just advised me to plan for twenty years I shall probably never see.

SHIRLEY. You've got to think of the future, but live for today.

VICTOR. You're never lost for an answer, are you? Who trained you? Ah, now I know what your father is. He's a barrister.

SHIRLEY. No, he's not. He's a—don't laugh.

VICTOR. Why should I laugh?

SHIRLEY. People usually do.

VICTOR. No, I wouldn't dream of it. Really I wouldn't.

SHIRLEY (*deeply ashamed of it*) He's a parson.

VICTOR (*bursting out laughing*) Oh, my God, a parson! (*Controlling himself*) That was a near thing. I nearly committed an offence against the cloth.

SHIRLEY. Everybody reacts like that. Do you know, as soon as I told Giles he ran out to get a licence. (*She gets up and puts her arms round Victor*) Victor! What a super name! It suits you perfectly. Victor Victorious. Happy and glorious.

VICTOR. I'm not a bit happy and I'm absolutely no use to you. (*He moves* C) I'm inhibited by a dozen considerations, not the least being the fact that I'm poaching on my son's preserves. I felt badly enough when I accidentally wrecked his model aircraft.

SHIRLEY. Giles and I are going to separate anyway.

VICTOR. Are you really?

SHIRLEY. One of us will have to find a new pad. And we'll share out the things we bought together.

VICTOR. How very sad. Three teacups each.

SHIRLEY. So you needn't worry about Giles. And I can take a couple of weeks off any time.

VICTOR. What date is it today?

SHIRLEY. May the twenty-fifth—no, it's the twenty-sixth because it's tomorrow now.

VICTOR (*moving to Shirley*) Soon be June. My favourite month. Strawberries, roses, new potatoes.

SHIRLEY. This is no time to talk about potatoes.

VICTOR. Well, it brings me back to earth. June and you. What a tempting combination. But no! (*He moves* C)

SHIRLEY. Are you turning me down?

VICTOR. With much regret.

SHIRLEY. Then what was it all about? All that. Just now. What was it?

VICTOR. It was very nice. (*After a pause*) Thank you.

SHIRLEY. What did it mean?

VICTOR. You read so much into everything. A smile. A kiss. One's terrified to say good morning. (*He moves* R)

SHIRLEY (*deeply hurt and angry*) Go away.

VICTOR (*moving to her*) Shirley, you're not angry, are you?

SHIRLEY. I'm disgusted. You're a fake and a fraud. (*She cries*)

VICTOR. Now you really mustn't cry.

SHIRLEY (*hiding her face*) I'm not crying. Go away.

VICTOR. Shirley . . .

SHIRLEY. *Go away!* Go away.

VICTOR (*moving to the door down* L) Keep your voice down. If I could just . . .

SHIRLEY. Go away!

VICTOR. I've gone, I've gone.

(VICTOR *exits down* L *and switches on hall bracket.* SHIRLEY *settles down to sleep.* GILES *enters down* L *in his pyjamas*)

SHIRLEY. It's too late now.

GILES. What?

SHIRLEY (*sitting up*) Oh, it's you.

GILES. Who did you think it was?

SHIRLEY. You, of course. What do you want that you can't have?

GILES. I came to see if you were comfortable.

SHIRLEY. How kind.

GILES. Because you can come back now, if you're not.

SHIRLEY. You promised you wouldn't try anything.

GILES. I wish I hadn't now. You almost did me irreparable damage.

SHIRLEY. You asked for it. Drunken beast.

GILES. I had one small Scotch.

SHIRLEY. You tried to rape me.

GILES. I only wanted to re-establish cordial relations.

SHIRLEY. Cordial or conjugal? Whichever it was you went the wrong way about it. You've got a primitive approach, that's your trouble—you're limited.

GILES (*moving* C) What d'you want? A set of variations?

SHIRLEY. I'd like some imagination, some tenderness and some consideration.

GILES. In that order?

SHIRLEY. Simultaneously.

GILES. While working the record-player with my right foot, I suppose. (*He demonstrates*)

SHIRLEY. Yes, and peeling grapes with your left.

GILES. D'you know, I've been thinking.

SHIRLEY. What with?

GILES. D'you know what's wrong with us?

SHIRLEY. I know what's wrong with you.

GILES (*moving to Shirley*) We've been putting the cart before the horse.

SHIRLEY. What is the lad raving about?

GILES (*sitting on the chaise-longue*) We ought to get married. Sign the contract.

SHIRLEY. Listen, when I get married I want to be cherished and protected and provided for. I'm not interested in living on a hairline budget. Knitting socks made out of unravelled old pullovers which were made out of old socks in the first place.

Giles. Other couples manage on one pay packet.

Shirley. Sure. The simple life. Do you know, I knew a girl who used to cream her face with margarine?

Giles. Didn't her husband love her just the same?

Shirley. Not after she grew a beard.

(*They both enjoy the joke*)

Giles. You know, you wouldn't have to spend so much on clothes if you stayed at home. And you could take the time to cook economical dishes.

Shirley. Oh, I'd love that, Giles. That really does appeal to me. Super. Lucky me. Forget it.

Giles. I'll help.

Shirley. You—you couldn't even carry the bucket down to the bin. Now clear off. I want to sleep. (*She pushes him off the chaise-longue*)

Giles. I'll stay here. You can have the bed.

Shirley (*rising and moving to the door down* L) I'll grab that opportunity before you change your mind. (*Pausing at the door*) Would it be all right if I have a bath?

Giles. Yes, as long as you don't sing.

Shirley. I don't feel like singing. This has been one hell of a night.

(Shirley *exits down* L. Giles *switches off the lights and tries to get comfortable on the chaise-longue. He is taller than Shirley and has some difficulty. After a few moments* Victor's *voice is heard outside the door down* L)

Victor (*off*) Shirley?

(Giles *throws the blanket over his head.* Victor *enters, wearing just his dressing-gown, and moves behind the chaise-longue*)

Shirley? I couldn't sleep either. I feel oddly guilty. Though it wasn't all my doing, you must admit that. Don't feel too badly about it, darling. It's happened to me before—it's a thing almost outside my control. It always happens the same way. A smile, a compliment or two. . . . You're not still crying, are you? (*He puts a comforting hand on the concealed body*)

(Giles *reacts violently*)

I'll stay for a little while. (*He sits on the back of the chaise-longue*) But it wouldn't do for anyone to find us like this. Still, Joan's in a coma and Giles is in the bath. His favourite refuge. That and the other little room. (*He laughs*) Poor boy. He's still got a lot to learn. I'd like to kiss you again.

(*The body moves convulsively*)

No, quite right. Three times is enough on a warm night like this.

Shirley, say something. Come on. Well, give me your hand. Come on, where's your hand? (*He feels for her hand under the blanket*) I say, you've got a powerful grip for a *girl* . . .

(VICTOR's *voice rises to a high pitch as* GILES *grips his hand.* GILES *sits up, causing* VICTOR *to fall off the back of the chaise-longue*)

Giles! I thought you were . . . (*He points upwards*)

GILES. Obviously.

VICTOR. Did I wake you?

GILES. I wasn't asleep.

VICTOR. Not at first.

GILES. Not at all.

VICTOR. Do you mean that you deliberately . . . (*He switches on the main lights*)

GILES. That's right.

VICTOR (*moving* C; *indignantly*) But you knew damn well I wasn't talking to you.

GILES. I hoped as much when you offered to kiss me. Unless you include perverted incest among the conventions you live by.

VICTOR. Oh, lord.

GILES. Now I know why you were so anxious to keep us apart. So that you could have a crack at Shirley yourself.

VICTOR. There was nothing premeditated about this.

GILES. You're not denying it, then?

VICTOR (*moving to the door down* L) Keep your voice down. You'll rouse the whole house.

GILES. *I want to!*

VICTOR (*moving* C) You're getting all worked up over a—a flea-bite.

GILES (*rising*) A flea-bite? Three times? Three times in under an hour. You're telling me I've got a lot to learn.

VICTOR. Are you raving mad? What d'you think I am?

GILES. A living testimony to halibut oil and malt. Granny says you never missed a day.

VICTOR. Go and ask Shirley what happened. Or rather, what didn't.

GILES. Shirley is having a bath. (*He opens the door and calls*) Shirley!

VICTOR (*moving to Giles*) Giles! (*Very quietly*) It's almost two o'clock.

GILES. You're very anxious to keep it dark, aren't you?

VICTOR (*moving* C) I'm trying to stop you from making an idiot of yourself.

GILES. You've already made me an idiot. By cuckolding me.

VICTOR. You can't be a cuckold if you're not married.

GILES. You think the fact that we're not married makes it open season.

VICTOR. I'm sorry, Giles.

GILES. Like hell you are. Poor Giles. I heard that. Poor unsuspecting nit. Up to his neck in hot water while I'm making his girl.

VICTOR. I wasn't. (*He sits in the armchair*) Look, you'd better have a drink.

GILES. I couldn't swallow anything you'd paid for. It would stick in my throat.

VICTOR. I'll tell Joan there'll only be four for breakfast.

GILES (*moving to Victor*) You think it's funny, don't you? You find everything so damned amusing. Why my girl, dammit? Why pick mine? There are plenty of other fish—if you're that way inclined.

VICTOR. This one happened to swim straight towards me.

(SHIRLEY *enters, wearing a towel sarong fashion, and moves in front of the chaise-longue*)

SHIRLEY. What's going on?

VICTOR. There's been some confusion.

GILES. I'll say.

VICTOR. I came downstairs—to see—if you were all right.

SHIRLEY (*still angry with him*) Oh, yes?

VICTOR. Giles was lying there, doggo, and I spoke to him, that is, I spoke to you—well, I thought it was you . . .

SHIRLEY. What did you say to him?

VICTOR. You can imagine, can't you? (*He rises*)

SHIRLEY. Oh, what a scream! (*She begins to laugh*)

VICTOR. Unfortunately, Giles didn't see the joke.

SHIRLEY. No, he wouldn't, would he. I wish I could have seen his face. And yours. Whoops, my toga's slipping.

GILES. You're in a dizzy mood, aren't you?

SHIRLEY. Who wouldn't be? (*She moves between Victor and Giles*) Cadwallader *père et fils*. Shall we dance?

(*She begins to dance.* MARTIN *enters down* L *wearing pyjamas and dressing-gown*)

MARTIN (*reasonably enough*) What's going on?

VICTOR. We're just having a party. (*He moves down* R)

(SHIRLEY *sits in the armchair*)

GILES (*kneeling on the chaise-longue*) He did the same to you, didn't he?

MARTIN. Who? What?

GILES. He dived in and harpooned your fish.

MARTIN (*closing the door and moving behind the chaise-longue*) Are you having a nightmare?

GILES. Listen, I came down here so that Shirley could get some rest.

SHIRLEY. Oooh!

GILES. The bed wasn't wide enough and we kept bumping into each other.

SHIRLEY. Understatement of the year.

GILES. And I was lying on the chaise-longue.
SHIRLEY. What a wicked name for a Victorian sofa!
GILES. With a blanket over my head—(*rising and moving* C, *pointing at Victor*) when my father came slinking in, in that dressing-gown.
VICTOR (*sitting on the stool* R) It was a Christmas present from your mother.
GILES. It's got a sinful look about it.
VICTOR. What a funny old word. Sin's out, you know. Fini. Kaput.
GILES. Honour isn't. (*He moves on to the rostrum up* C)
VICTOR. You make up your own rules as you go along.
MARTIN (*moving up to Giles*) How did you know who it was if you had the blanket over your head?
GILES. I recognized his voice.
MARTIN. What did he say?

(SHIRLEY *and* VICTOR *move to the door down* L)

GILES. He said "Shirley", so naturally I waited to see what he was going to do next. Where are you going?
SHIRLEY ⎱ (*together*) ⎰ To bed.
VICTOR ⎰   ⎱
GILES (*moving in front of the armchair*) There you are, you see!
VICTOR (*moving* C) Now, Giles, you really must stop this.

(SHIRLEY *moves to the end of the chaise-longue.* JOAN *enters in her nightdress, dazed and blinking*)

JOAN. What is this? A pyjama party?
VICTOR. You know you shouldn't get up when you've taken a sleeping pill.

(VICTOR *helps Joan to sit on the chaise-longue.* MARTIN *moves down stage,* L *of Giles*)

JOAN. There was such a racket going on. (*She catches sight of Shirley*) I could lend you a proper robe.
SHIRLEY. I've got one upstairs, thank you.
JOAN. Then I suggest you put it on. Before you catch a cold. Or something.

(SHIRLEY *exits down* L. JOAN *sees Giles and Martin standing together*)

What's the matter with those two?
VICTOR (*moving behind the chaise-longue*) They've got something in common, darling. A dirty great grudge against me.
JOAN. What are you talking about?
GILES (*to Martin*) Should I tell her?
MARTIN. It's got nothing to do with me.
VICTOR. That's never stopped you from shoving your oar in before, has it?
MARTIN (*to Giles*) But I would if I were you.
GILES (*moving to Joan*) Dad and Shirley have been having it off.

(JOAN *begins to giggle, then bursts into laughter*)

JOAN. You'll never believe what I thought he said.

GILES. I did—say what you thought I said.

JOAN. What?

GILES. I can't put it any plainer.

VICTOR. That's not for want of trying.

JOAN. But when? Where? How?

GILES. Just before you came down. On this.

JOAN. On the chaise-longue?

VICTOR. You must admit it's improbable.

MARTIN. It's not impossible.

VICTOR. How do you know? Have you ever tried?

MARTIN. Certainly not.

VICTOR (*moving below the armchair*) No, it's all theory with you, isn't it?

JOAN. Victor, is this true?

VICTOR (*beginning to lose his temper*) Of course it isn't true.

GILES (*interrupting*) It is. It is. He told me himself and now he's trying to deny it. He told me himself.

JOAN. Don't shout, darling. Victor, this time you've gone too far. Far too far—far too . . .

(SHIRLEY *enters down* L *wearing a shorty nightdress and frilled jacket*)

I think I preferred the towel.

SHIRLEY (*crossing* R *and sitting on the stool*) What's the verdict.

VICTOR. Guilty, with no right of appeal. Only you can save me.

SHIRLEY. How?

VICTOR. By telling them that I'm innocent, of course. Go on, tell them.

SHIRLEY. But you're not, are you?

VICTOR. What?

SHIRLEY. Not really.

VICTOR. What are you trying to do?

SHIRLEY. Be honest.

GILES. You see. You see.

JOAN. You! You never let anything stand in your way. Not even the fact that Giles is your son. Or rather, you *think* he is.

JOAN *falls forward on the chaise-longue, deeply asleep.* VICTOR *stares first at Joan, then at Giles, finally at Martin.* VICTOR *approaches Martin threateningly, and* MARTIN *retreats, as—*

the CURTAIN *falls*

ACT III

SCENE—*The same. The following morning.*

When the CURTAIN *rises,* VICTOR *is lying, completely covered by a blanket, on the chaise-longue.* MARTIN *enters down* L, *dressed, sees the figure and very gently turns back a corner of the blanket to discover who it is. Seeing it is Victor,* MARTIN *grins to himself, opens the curtains, and exits to the kitchen. After a few moments* VICTOR *stirs and rises. His legs are stiff from the uncomfortable position in which he has been sleeping. He is still wearing just his dressing-gown.* SHIRLEY *enters up* R *dressed and full of energy.*

SHIRLEY. Good morning.
VICTOR. Is it?
SHIRLEY. Did you spend the night down here?
VICTOR. What was left of it.
SHIRLEY. Nearly everybody seems to have had a go on the chaise-longue.
VICTOR (*sitting up*) Everybody thinks we had a go on it.
SHIRLEY (*sitting in the armchair*) You shouldn't have come down again, should you?
VICTOR. No, I shouldn't, should I.

(MARTIN *enters from the kitchen, wearing a blue striped apron and carrying a tea towel*)

Ah, Martin. The hero of Muswell Hill. Some achieve paternity, some have paternity thrust upon them.
MARTIN. You're awake.
VICTOR. Full marks for observation.
SHIRLEY. Good morning.
MARTIN (*moving to Shirley*) Good morning. You're an early bird. Would you like tea or coffee?
SHIRLEY. Whatever you're making.
MARTIN. I can make both, either or neither.
SHIRLEY. I'd love some tea.
MARTIN. Strongish?
SHIRLEY. Stand the spoon up in it.
MARTIN (*moving above the chaise-longue*) Coffee for you, old man? (*He picks up the blanket*)
VICTOR. Thank you. You and I must have a little talk, mustn't we? There are certain matters which will have to be thrashed out.
MARTIN (*cheerfully*) Not before breakfast, old man. Not on an empty stomach. (*He picks up the pillow and moves on to the rostrum*)
VICTOR. Why have you suddenly started calling me "old man"?
MARTIN. We always refer to you as the old man, Joanie and I. (*Moving to the kitchen*) That's why.

SHIRLEY. Do you want any help?

MARTIN. Oh, no, thank you. It's rather a small kitchen. Not enough room for two, unless they happen to be on fairly intimate terms.

(MARTIN *exits to the kitchen*)

VICTOR. What was that supposed to mean? He and Joan practically *live* in there.

SHIRLEY. Perhaps that's what it's supposed to mean.

VICTOR. He's never spoken to me like this before.

SHIRLEY. He probably didn't know that he'd pipped you at the post before.

VICTOR. What a revolting way of describing a matter which has not yet been proved.

SHIRLEY (*moving to Victor*) Haven't you asked your wife a few pertinent questions?

VICTOR. I haven't had the chance yet, but there's a couple I'd like to ask you. Why didn't you back me up last night, and tell the truth? I felt such an idiot, standing there, without a leg to stand on.

SHIRLEY. You know damn well you had adultery on your mind last night.

VICTOR. I've got adultery on my mind every night. The point is, I abstained.

SHIRLEY (*moving above the chaise-longue and sitting on the back*) Only because you didn't feel safe. You wouldn't have abstained if we'd been in an hotel room, or if we'd been lying at the bottom of a punt among the willows, or if we'd been hidden by long grass on a hot summer's night . . .

VICTOR. That's enough, thank you very much. Inflaming my imagination on a Sunday morning. And you a parson's daughter.

SHIRLEY. Well, admit it, then. Go on, admit it.

VICTOR. Shush. Big ears is in the galley. I grant you, in other surroundings I might have succumbed to your undeniable — ecclesiastical charm. After all, I'm only human.

SHIRLEY. Yes—and some of us are more human than others.

VICTOR. Let's stick to the point. In this case I'm blameless—stainless.

SHIRLEY. And all for what? You've been hanged for a sheep when you haven't even stolen a lamb, and since everybody thinks that you did, it's not going to make a haporth of difference if we do.

VICTOR (*looking at the kitchen door to make sure Martin is not listening*) Do what?

SHIRLEY. Go away together. Next month. June. Remember? Hey, are you sure you're not Giles' father?

VICTOR. I feel more like his grandfather this morning.

SHIRLEY. Because you're awfully like him in some ways. He's thick.

VICTOR. Thick?

SHIRLEY. Slow on the uptake.

VICTOR. I've got a lot on my mind.

SHIRLEY. Yes. When are you going to ask your wife what she meant?

VICTOR. When I'm ready. After all, the boy was conceived twenty years ago. Twenty minutes more won't make much difference, will it?

SHIRLEY. But it's important.

VICTOR. I don't need you to tell me that.

SHIRLEY. Then what do you need me for?

(VICTOR *looks at her*)

Would you like me to go?

VICTOR. No, I want you to stay. I might need your moral support, or something . . .

SHIRLEY (*rising*) It must have shaken you a bit.

VICTOR. That's one way of putting it.

SHIRLEY (*wandering* C) Not very tactful of her. In front of everybody.

VICTOR. I don't suppose she was feeling very tactful. Thanks mainly to you.

SHIRLEY. You ought to be thanking me for helping you to find out. You wouldn't have known, otherwise.

VICTOR. Perhaps not.

SHIRLEY (*moving above the chaise-longue*) You've been rearing a little cuckoo in your nest.

VICTOR. I do wish you wouldn't refer to my son as a little cuckoo.

SHIRLEY. He's not your son.

(GILES *bursts in from the garden, his teeth chattering. He is still in pyjamas, and is wrapped in a rug*)

Where have you been?

GILES (*sitting in the armchair*) In the summer-house.

VICTOR. What, all night?

GILES. What was left of it.

VICTOR. But the window's broken and the door won't shut properly.

GILES. Now he tells me!

VICTOR. Why did you go out there?

GILES. I wanted some fresh untainted air.

SHIRLEY (*moving to Giles*) And you got some, didn't you? Don't you look terrible? God, you look awful. (*She sits on the stool* R)

(MARTIN *enters with the breakfast trolley*)

MARTIN (*moving up* C) Here we are! Breakfast is ready. (*He rushes to Giles and puts his hand on Giles' head*) My boy, what's the matter? You're shaking. (*He returns to the trolley*)

GILES. You'd shake if you'd spent the night in a rustic refrigerator.

(MARTIN *pours Giles a cup of coffee*)

SHIRLEY. It's practically summer.

GILES. It is in here, but outside the temperature fell to ten below and the dawn came up like thunder.

SHIRLEY. Nobody asked you to fling yourself out under the stars in a fit of temperament.

VICTOR (*taking the cup from Martin and moving to Giles*) Here, drink this.

(GILES *turns his head away*)

Go on. Don't be so bloody obstinate.

GILES. I get that from you.

MARTIN. You don't, you know.

(MARTIN *exits to the kitchen*)

VICTOR. Exit St George with flag flying. Here. (*He gives Giles the coffee*)

GILES (*taking the cup*) What do I call you now?

VICTOR. What would you like to call me?

SHIRLEY. You're laying yourself wide open.

VICTOR. In any case, I shall go on calling you Giles. After all, I chose your name. (*He pours himself a cup of coffee*)

GILES. In a few short hours I've learned that my uncle's my father, my father's my rival, and my bird's as unreliable as my motor-bike. My mother has been hiding a guilty secret from the world, and on top of that, I think I've got frostbite.

(VICTOR *wanders below the chaise-longue*)

SHIRLEY. Oh, you poor bastard.

VICTOR. He's not, you know. His mother was married.

SHIRLEY. Yes, but to the wrong man. (*She goes to the trolley and helps herself to a cup of tea*)

GILES. I shall have to rethink all my relationships.

VICTOR (*sitting on the chaise-longue*) You're lucky. I seem to have lost half of mine.

SHIRLEY. I wish my mother would suddenly spring something like that on me. "I'll tell you now, Shirley, now that you're old enough to understand. Your real father is——

VICTOR. —the Bishop.

(VICTOR *and* SHIRLEY *find this hysterically funny.* GILES *is shocked*)

GILES. You think it's all a great joke, don't you?

VICTOR. Well, you've got to laugh, haven't you—I hope you realize you've brought this whole unfortunate business on yourself.

(SHIRLEY *sits on the stool* R)

GILES. Why, what did I do?

VICTOR. It's more what you didn't do. If you'd come out from underneath that blanket last night and sat up like a good boy and said, "It's me, Daddy," your mother wouldn't have gone clean off her chump and Martin wouldn't be behaving like a dog with two tails.

GILES (*rising and moving to Victor*) You mean it wouldn't have mattered as long as nobody found out.

VICTOR. You've got it.

GILES. I don't want it.

VICTOR. It's the general rule in business, politics, love and war. Let sleeping dogs lie, and don't turn up stones in case you find something nasty underneath.

GILES. Well, I did find something nasty, very nasty.

(GILES *exits down* L)

VICTOR. Poor kid. I wouldn't have hurt him for the world.

SHIRLEY (*moving to the chaise-longue and sitting* R *of Victor*) He'll find another girl.

VICTOR. That's what I used to say to Martin—find somebody else. But did he? No.

SHIRLEY (*joining in*) No.

VICTOR. Why go to the trouble and expense of supporting a wife of his own, when he could so easily borrow mine.

SHIRLEY. Yes. Now, where shall we go?

VICTOR. Go?

SHIRLEY. In June. (*She kneels by Victor*) I do wish you'd concentrate. I love you.

VICTOR. Do you really?

SHIRLEY. Aren't you getting a little bit fond of me?

VICTOR. I think you're sweet. In fact, if I were a bit younger . . .

SHIRLEY. I don't want you any younger. You're just right. Same age as my father. Why don't you come up to Yorkshire?

VICTOR. Yorkshire? Whatever for?

SHIRLEY. It's very bracing.

VICTOR. Alone with you it'd be bracing anywhere.

SHIRLEY. Super.

VICTOR. I don't see why I should go charging half-way up England. I like it here.

SHIRLEY. Why don't you get rid of the others, and we'll stay here?

VICTOR. That's the best idea you've had yet.

SHIRLEY. You're waking up now, aren't you.

VICTOR. Yes, but this is only supposing.

SHIRLEY (*rising and moving behind the chaise-longue*) Supposing what? What more do you want? Proof positive? Chapter and verse?

VICTOR. I still can't believe that Joan and Martin . . .

(MARTIN *enters with a breakfast tray, humming*)

Where are you going with that?

MARTIN. I'm taking it up to Joanie.

VICTOR. Isn't she still in bed?

MARTIN. Yes.

VICTOR (*taking the tray*) I'll take it up to Joanie.

MARTIN. As you wish, but aren't you rather shutting the stable door?

SHIRLEY. There's your answer.

VICTOR. You know, you're becoming dangerous. After lying

dormant for twenty years like a left-over land-mine you've begun
to tick.

(MARTIN *retreats up stage*)

I shall have to dismantle his fuse.

SHIRLEY (*taking the tray*) Let me take it. Your wife might throw
it at you. (*She moves down* L)

VICTOR. She might throw it at you.

SHIRLEY. I'll just pop it down by the door.

VICTOR. Clever.

SHIRLEY. Hey, wouldn't she let you sleep with her last night?

VICTOR (*sitting on the chaise-longue*) Let's say I was dismissed from
active service.

(SHIRLEY *exits down* L. MARTIN *empties ashtrays from the mantelpiece
and the* C *table, into the waste-paper basket beside the desk*)

(*In a high-pitched voice*) What a busy, busy bee you are, Martin. Never
an idle moment.

MARTIN (*clearing the ashtray from the drinks cabinet*) I like to make
myself useful.

VICTOR. So I gather!

MARTIN. I think you should have someone to look at that dish-
washer of yours. It's making funny noises.

(MARTIN *exits to the kitchen with the basket. After a moment he returns
with the basket empty, and a duster. He puts the basket back beside the
desk.*)

VICTOR. That's not the only thing we've got to look at, is it?
(*Rising and replacing his cup on the trolley*) I don't care if it's doing the
Eighteen-Twelve Overture. You're very cool.

MARTIN (*dusting the ashtray on the mantelpiece*) We must keep our
heads for Joanie's sake. For my son's sake.

VICTOR (*moving to Martin*) Your son?

MARTIN. Yes.

VICTOR. He doesn't look like you.

MARTIN (*dusting the ashtray on the* C *table*) He doesn't look like you,
either.

VICTOR. He takes after Joan's family. There's a resemblance to
her Uncle Henry.

MARTIN. I've never met him.

VICTOR. You're lucky. You could have had a nasty shock.

(SHIRLEY *enters* L *and sits on the back of the chaise-longue*)

Is she still asleep?

SHIRLEY. She seems to be, unless she's pretending.

VICTOR (*moving down* L) I'm going to get to the bottom of this—
but first I'm going to have a shower and a shave and make myself
pink, smooth and beautiful.

(VICTOR *blows Martin a kiss and exits down* L)

SHIRLEY. You're beautiful now. (*She blows Victor a kiss. To Martin*) He's basically insecure.

(VICTOR *half returns*)

VICTOR. You could be right.

(VICTOR *exits.* MARTIN *laughs to himself and dusts the* C *table*)

SHIRLEY. You're enjoying yourself, aren't you? Crowing over Victor like a farmyard rooster?

MARTIN. For years Victor has regarded me as a bad joke. Now it's my turn to laugh at him.

(JOAN, *still in her nightgown, makes a surreptitious entrance from the kitchen*)

JOAN. Where's Victor?

MARTIN. In the bathroom.

SHIRLEY (*moving down* L) Getting ready to put a few pertinent questions to you.

JOAN (*moving* C) Never mind about that. What did you and Victor get up to last night?

SHIRLEY. You'd better ask him yourself.

(SHIRLEY *exits down* L)

JOAN. Sweet girl—I'd like to kill her. Victor's hopping mad, I suppose.

MARTIN. You'll have to face him sooner or later.

JOAN (*moving to the armchair and sitting*) Oh, let it be later. As late as possible. Whatever possessed me to drop a clanger like that last night?

MARTIN. I thought you said it on purpose.

JOAN. Good heavens, no. If I'd been responsible for what I was saying, I wouldn't have said it. But I was half doped, and furious with Victor.

MARTIN (*squatting by the armchair*) Small wonder.

JOAN. Oh, not because he was playing around. He can't help that. One might as well be angry with a cat because it chases birds.

MARTIN. Why then?

JOAN. Because of Giles, stupid.

(MARTIN, *hurt, turns his head away*)

Oh, I'm sorry, Martin. I'm a bit edgy this morning. Get me a cigarette, please?

(MARTIN *takes a cigarette from the table* C, *lights it, and hands it to Joan*)

When I think how long it took me to persuade Giles to come down and see us! The letters. The phone calls. And then, when he gets here, Victor has to ruin everything by muscling in on his girl!

MARTIN. Well, a tomcat doesn't discriminate between one bird and the next.

(GILES *enters down* L, *now dressed*)

JOAN (*rising*) Hello, my darling.

GILES. 'Morning.

MARTIN (*moving the trolley* L) The boy spent the night in the summer-house.

(MARTIN *exits to the kitchen with the trolley*)

JOAN. Poor lamb. It couldn't have been very comfortable.

GILES (*moving up* L) I had to go somewhere.

JOAN. How on earth did you manage with all those creepy crawlies out there?

(MARTIN *enters*)

GILES (*looking at Martin*) No worse than with all the creepy crawlies in here.

JOAN (*putting her hand on his arm*) It's been a rotten homecoming for you.

GILES (*shrugging off her hand*) Would you mind not pawing me about.

JOAN. You behave as though I was the one who'd been bouncing on the chaise-longue.

GILES. It's not where you did your bouncing that concerns me. It's when and with whom. I didn't expect that sort of thing from you, Mother. (*He moves down* R *and glances through the magazines on top of the television set*)

JOAN (*following him*) What right have you to judge me? You come here flaunting your sexual freedom and laying down ultimatums about bedrooms.

(GILES *moves up* L. JOAN *follows him*)

You of all people, with your new morality, should be able to over-look one small lapse.

GILES. Not when that small lapse turns out to be me.

(GILES *exits up* L)

JOAN (*moving below the armchair*) Is that fair? He's in favour of love, liberty and licence for himself, but I'm expected to toe the line.

MARTIN. He shouldn't have turned on you like that.

JOAN. I must tell him.

MARTIN (*moving to stop her*) No, don't do that.

JOAN. But I must.

(SHIRLEY *appears in the doorway down* L)

MARTIN. What about Victor?

JOAN. He'll have to be told sooner or later.

MARTIN. But I've hardly got going yet.

JOAN. What have you been doing?

SHIRLEY (*moving to the chaise-longue*) He's been playing it up for all he's worth. (*She sits*)

JOAN (*sitting in the armchair*) Oh, my God.

MARTIN (*moving to the window up* L) I've never seen Victor so shaken. It's marvellous, marvellous.

JOAN. I'm glad I've brightened up the week-end for you.

SHIRLEY. Isn't it true, then, about you and Martin?

JOAN. My maiden name, at a time when a maiden name meant exactly what it sounds like, was Page. But since I changed it for a mouthful of Cadwallader, I've never been unfaithful.

MARTIN (*moving to Joan*) Now she'll tell Victor.

SHIRLEY. No, I won't. I promise you. I won't breathe a word. But isn't it a bit unkind?

JOAN. Unkind? I hope you don't imagine that you're the first, or that you'll be the last.

MARTIN. There was Judith, Cynthia——

JOAN. Yes.

MARTIN. —Valerie——

JOAN. I haven't asked you to compile a list.

MARTIN. —and that one who was mentally retarded . . .

JOAN. She wasn't mentally retarded. She was shy.

MARTIN (*moving to the fireplace*) Well, it's your life, Joanie, but as I see it, you've got to make a stand somewhere. If you let him get away with it this time, where is it going to end?

JOAN. Oh, Martin, he's not as bad as all that. He's simply promiscuous.

MARTIN. So let him suffer for a while. Do him good.

JOAN. He probably doesn't believe it anyway.

MARTIN. He does, Joanie. He thinks that I'm responsible for Giles.

JOAN. Listen, Victor's short on morals, but he's no fool.

SHIRLEY. Martin was very convincing.

MARTIN. After all, it's not so hard to believe, is it, darling? (*Moving above the armchair to* L *of Joan*) We have been very close.

SHIRLEY. Ah ha!

JOAN. It's not what you think.

(GILES *enters up* L)

Giles, do you feel better?

GILES. I've got Elsie ticking over spasmodically.

SHIRLEY. Two hundred miles in spasms. I can hardly wait!

GILES (*sitting on the chaise-longue*) Are you coming to Manchester with me, or staying here with your elderly lover?

(VICTOR, *dressed, enters from the kitchen and moves* C)

VICTOR (*to Joan*) Good morning, Joan.

MARTIN (*to Joan*) Victor has something to ask you.

VICTOR. I don't need you to make an opening announcement.

MARTIN. Go ahead then.

VICTOR. I'll go ahead without your blowing your bloody whistle. (*To Joan*) What did you mean last night when . . .

(JOAN *rises and moves to the door down* L)

Where do you think you're going?

JOAN. I've got to get dressed.

VICTOR. You can get dressed later.

JOAN. If we're going to have a row, I mean a discussion, I'm not having it while you're all spruced up and I've just fallen out of bed. It puts me at a disadvantage. (*She turns to exit*)

VICTOR. If you go through that door, we're finished! Finished!

(JOAN *turns and heads briskly for the kitchen door*)

Or that one!

(JOAN *exits through the window up* L *and enters through the window up* R)

MARTIN. Joanie! Joanie! (*He motions to her to stand* R *of him*)

JOAN (*doing so*) Martin . . .

(MARTIN *protects her, standing down* L *of the armchair*)

VICTOR. Oh, St George is at it again. Now I want to know.

JOAN. We'll talk about it over lunch.

VICTOR. Oh, yes. Am I the father of my son, pass the mint sauce, please. Giles . . .

JOAN. Leave him alone, Victor. He's upset.

VICTOR. Whose fault is that?

JOAN. As much yours as mine.

VICTOR. Giles.

GILES. Yes?

VICTOR. Ask your mother who your father is.

GILES. I'm too old to swop fathers in midstream.

VICTOR. Does it matter so much to you? After all, we've never been on the best of terms.

GILES. I hated you. Now I can't any more.

VICTOR. Why not?

GILES. The whole joy's gone out of it somehow.

VICTOR. You can get to hate your new father. Nothing could be easier.

MARTIN. I think perhaps you ought to know that Joanie spent the night with me.

VICTOR. When?

MARTIN. When she should have been with her mother.

JOAN. Martin, you promised.

VICTOR. Do you mean you weren't with your mother, in the Isle of Wight?

MARTIN (*shaking his head*) No, with me, in Notting Hill Gate. (*He squats in front of Joan*)

VICTOR (*pushing Martin aside*) Is this true?

JOAN. Yes. But it was only once.

SHIRLEY (*laughing*) Only once. Sorry, that struck me as being rather funny.

VICTOR (*rising*) It struck me as being mighty incredible. Am I expected to believe that he's been hanging around here ever since in the hope of a return engagement?

MARTIN. It was more than once, darling.

JOAN (*rising and moving below the armchair*) Stop it, Martin. It's all your fault, Victor, for being so difficult.

VICTOR. When have I been difficult?

MARTIN. Have you forgotten that Joanie went home to her mother five times in the first twelve months of your marriage?

VICTOR. So she said.

MARTIN. Exactly.

GILES. Am I to understand that either of them might be my father?

JOAN. I suppose so.

VICTOR. You suppose so. Don't you know?

JOAN. Not for certain.

SHIRLEY. I call that careless.

VICTOR. I call it adultery.

JOAN. Don't take it too badly, darling. You're the man most likely to . . .

VICTOR. It's like Russian roulette. My blushing bride hops into bed with the best man, and I'm the one most likely to . . .

JOAN. We didn't go to bed.

VICTOR. What did you do, then? Have it on the hearth rug?

(MARTIN *moves in front of the fireplace*)

JOAN. I wish you wouldn't go on about it in front of the children.

VICTOR (*moving behind the chaise-longue*) Children! They've forgotten more than I shall ever know. All right, how long have you been running two of us concurrently?

JOAN. It was only once.

SHIRLEY. Even once—when you're still really on your honeymoon.

GILES. Look who's talking.

SHIRLEY. I couldn't help falling in love. I'm very impressionable.

JOAN. It's all your fault, Giles.

GILES. What?

JOAN. If you had to bring a girl here, you should have kept your eye on her instead of leaving her lying around loose. You know what your father is.

GILES (*rising*) Well, I knew what he was. Now I don't even know if he is. I'm getting out of here. Sex is one thing, but reproduction's another.

(GILES *exits up* L)

JOAN. I hope you're satisfied. You can never resist seeing if the old charm still works. I don't know what I'd have done without Martin all these years. (*She moves to Martin*)

MARTIN (*meeting Joan below the armchair and comforting her*) Never mind, Joanie.

VICTOR. Apart from supplying money I seem to be completely redundant around here. Why don't you go with him?

JOAN. All right, I will. (*Crossing to the door down* L) I'll just get myself ready, Martin.

VICTOR. I'll open the door for you. (*He does so*)

(JOAN *exits down* L, *crying, and goes upstairs*)

MARTIN (*beginning to follow*) Hey, Joanie—Joanie . . . (*He clears his throat and looks enigmatic*)

VICTOR (*his mood changing to pleasant, almost gay*) Anything wrong?

(MARTIN *retreats below the armchair*)

I think this calls for a celebration.

MARTIN. Celebration?

VICTOR (*moving to the drinks*) Certainly. (*He pours two drinks*)

MARTIN (*watching him; puzzled*) If that drink's for me, not such a big one. You know my head.

VICTOR (*moving with the drink to Martin*) Come on, Martin. Be a devil for once. It's not every day you become a father, is it.

MARTIN (*taking the drink*) You're taking it awfully well.

VICTOR. It didn't come as a complete surprise.

MARTIN. No?

VICTOR. Not really. Drink up, Martin. Come on, straight down in one.

MARTIN. Oh, no, I couldn't.

VICTOR. Come on—to you—to Daddy.

(MARTIN *drinks*)

You were the best man at our wedding, Martin, and the best man won.

MARTIN. I'm sorry, Victor. (*He sits in the armchair*)

VICTOR. It's poetic justice, really. Joan was originally yours. (*He takes Martin's empty glass and gives him his own full one*)

MARTIN. Well, we were engaged, as I think I've said before.

VICTOR (*moving to the drinks cabinet*) Yes, you have said it before. Sometimes twice a week.

SHIRLEY. I think it's beautiful.

VICTOR. What is?

SHIRLEY. Martin's lifelong devotion.

VICTOR. Yes, but the incredible thing is that he got a son straight off! In one night! (*He returns to Martin with a bottle of Teacher's*) What a night that must have been, eh? A night to remember.

MARTIN (*the drink taking effect*) Yes, I've been trying to remember it.

VICTOR. It shouldn't be difficult, should it? It's the sort of thing that tends to stick in your mind a bit. (*With fake admiration*) You're a dark horse. Good old Martin. Have a drop of Teacher's.

MARTIN. No, I shouldn't.

VICTOR. Nonsense. You can't go through life saying, "I shouldn't." (*He refills Martin's glass*)

SHIRLEY. Don't give him any more.

MARTIN (*downs the whisky in one go*) One night you'd been absolutely beastly to Joanie.

VICTOR (*squatting beside Martin*) I'm a swine.

MARTIN. She turned to me for comfort.

VICTOR. Thank God she had you to turn to.

MARTIN. I remember we sat on the divan . . .

VICTOR. Yes?

MARTIN. She put her head on my shoulder.

VICTOR. Yes?

MARTIN. We were experimenting.

VICTOR. Experimenting?

MARTIN. With vodka. Somebody said that if you mixed milk and vodka together it didn't affect you.

VICTOR. And did it?

MARTIN. That's the part I've been trying to remember.

(JOAN *enters* L, *dressed in a suit and carrying her handbag*)

JOAN. I'm ready, Martin.

(MARTIN *looks at her and laughs*)

(*To Victor*) Have you been getting him drunk?

VICTOR. Nothing to do with me, darling. (*Rising and moving* C) I put the cork of the brandy bottle down and he licked it.

JOAN. You're looking jolly pleased with yourself.

VICTOR. Just trying to keep cheerful, that's all.

SHIRLEY. I must be going too. Good-bye. (*She offers to shake hands with Joan*)

JOAN (*refusing Shirley's hand and going to comfort Martin*) Good-bye. (*She puts her handbag on the chaise-longue*)

VICTOR (*to Shirley*) Good-bye. (*He shakes her hand*)

(SHIRLEY *exits down* L)

JOAN. How's she going to get back?

VICTOR. With Giles, I suppose.

JOAN. I'm leaving you for good this time.

VICTOR. Whose good—yours or mine?

JOAN. You're not taking me seriously. I'm extremely fond of Martin.

VICTOR. Aren't we all? We're all fond of Martin. Good old Martin. Have another drink, Martin?

(GILES *enters up* L)

GILES. Elsie's playing up again, so we'll have to go by train. (*To Victor*) Can you lend me some money?

VICTOR. Ask your father.

GILES. It seems funny somehow.

VICTOR. He's not laughing, is he?

GILES (*to Martin*) Can you lend me some money, please?

VICTOR. I must warn you, Martin. Giles uses the word "lend" rather loosely.
MARTIN (*slowly producing a purse*) What sum had you in mind?
GILES. About ten——

(MARTIN *offers four half-crowns*)

—pounds!
VICTOR (*moving* L *of Giles*) Fifteen would be better, of course.
GILES. Yes, it would.

(MARTIN *puts his money back in his purse and returns it to his pocket*)

VICTOR (*handing Giles two fivers*) Here you are, Giles.
GILES. Fifteen would be better.

(VICTOR *hands Giles a third note*)

Thanks very much. I'll owe it to you.

(MARTIN *moves down* L)

VICTOR. You always do. (*To Martin*) It'll take me a few days to get everything in order. I'll let you have the account as soon as I can, Martin.
MARTIN. What account?
VICTOR. To educating and rearing one son.
JOAN. Don't be ridiculous.
MARTIN (*moving behind the chaise-longue*) What?
VICTOR. It's common justice. There's a sizeable sum involved. I was totting it up while I was shaving. The school fees alone come to between three and four thousand pounds. Then there's clothes, books, food—you've noticed his rate of metabolism?
JOAN. Victor . . .
VICTOR. Then there was Joan's confinement. Private nursing home—two dozen red roses . . .
JOAN. How could you bring up the flowers you sent me?
VICTOR. You can't expect me to foot the bill for two dozen hot-house blooms in January—that I sent you for bearing another man's child.
JOAN. Victor, you're going too far.

(MARTIN *sits on the back of the chaise-longue and puts his apron on it*)

VICTOR. I wasn't the one who went too far. Costly business, repro-duction. Pram, push-chair, high chair, plastic potties. Tricycles, bicycles, electric train sets, Meccano—then there was the *Eagle*, and . . .
GILES. *Beano.*
VICTOR (*to Giles*) I used to love *Beano*—and innumerable tubes of Smarties.
GILES. I used to go mad for Smarties.
VICTOR. Then he had his tonsils removed—anaesthetist's fee was separate. (*To Giles*) Then your front teeth were straightened,

weren't they—(*to Victor*)—that's why he's got such a lovely smile. Go on, show him your smile.

(GILES *smiles broadly*)

JOAN. You're being absurd.

VICTOR. I won't expect a lump sum. It must be at least ten thousand pounds. I'll accept payment by instalments. No interest, Martin, if that's all right with you? Whether you'll think he's worth it is another matter. I had no choice. But I'd say he was beginning to show potential.

GILES. Is that what I've cost you?

VICTOR. Afraid so.

GILES. And I begrudge you one measly girl.

VICTOR. Think nothing of it, Giles. It's a form of savings, really. Now that Martin's going to pay it back.

MARTIN (*rising*) Yes, you've done a great deal for Giles, a great deal. Perhaps we could meet up one day next week and talk it over.

VICTOR. How about dinner—Wednesday?

MARTIN. I'd like that, Victor.

VICTOR (*smiling*) Good. Where will you take me?

MARTIN. I'll give you a ring, Victor. Yes, I'll give you a ring.

(MARTIN *exits down* L)

JOAN. You frightened him. (*She sits in the armchair*)

VICTOR (*moving behind the chaise-longue*) The thought of any real responsibility frightened him. (*He picks up Martin's apron from the chaise-longue*) Oh look, he's forgotten his pinny.

GILES. I still don't know who my father is.

JOAN. This one, of course. He of the complacent smile and the overbearing manner.

GILES. Oh, good. That's a relief.

VICTOR. Is it?

GILES. Not that I cared either way.

VICTOR. No, I'm sure you didn't.

GILES. But a chap likes to know where he stands.

JOAN. Your father's not called Victor for nothing. He always comes out on top.

VICTOR. You put that very nicely, darling.

GILES. We'd better get moving. See you soon.

JOAN. Good-bye, my darling. (*She kisses Giles*)

VICTOR (*holding open the door down* L) Don't leave it so long next time.

GILES. I'll ask Uncle Martin if he can give us a lift to Euston.

(GILES *exits down* L)

JOAN. You will forgive me for playing that awful joke on you, won't you, darling?

VICTOR (*sitting on the chaise-longue*) Of course I will. I like a good joke.

JOAN. Good. When everybody's gone we could drive over to Cookham for lunch.

VICTOR. Cookham. That'll be nice.

JOAN. Then I thought we might go on to Woodstock and see Molly.

VICTOR. Ah, dear old Molly. And the rest of the day will be our own, I suppose.

JOAN. More or less.

VICTOR. Hmmm. What about Martin?

JOAN. Well, if he wants to go back to town early, that's up to him.

VICTOR. I'd hate myself if anything happened to him after all that Scotch I gave him.

JOAN. Yes, perhaps we'd better persuade him to stay.

VICTOR. No, no, I wouldn't do that, no. Let him go back to town, darling, but why don't you drive him?

JOAN. What would you do?

VICTOR. I'll stay on here. Relax a little.

JOAN. No, no. I couldn't leave you on your own.

(GILES *enters down* L)

GILES. Uncle Martin is taking us with him. (*Calling off*) Shirley!

(GILES *exits through the windows up* R)

VICTOR. Giles is going in the car with him, darling.

JOAN. Hmm—maybe you're right, Victor.

VICTOR. Yes, you're such a good driver.

JOAN (*rising*) Oh, darling, do you really think so?

VICTOR. You know I do.

JOAN (*moving* L) I'll get my things.

VICTOR. Yes, you get your things.

JOAN. I'll drive you all back to town.

(JOAN *exits down* L. MARTIN *appears in the doorway down* L *with a zip bag*)

MARTIN. Are you quite sure you don't mind, Victor?

VICTOR. No, no, I'm not a possessive man, and I trust you, Martin.

(GILES *enters up* R)

GILES. Shirley's gone and the bike's gone.

VICTOR. Can she ride that thing?

GILES. Yes, but the silly little ass won't get very far.

VICTOR. If you hurry up you might catch her.

GILES. Yes. Come on, Uncle Martin.

(GILES *exits down* L)

MARTIN. Your mother's driving.

(MARTIN *exits down* L)

GILES (*off*) Come on, Mum!

(JOAN *enters down* L *carrying two bags*)

JOAN. I'm coming. (*To Victor*) I'll ring you, darling.
VICTOR (*rising*) Do that.
JOAN. What about your lunch?
VICTOR. There's some cold lamb in the fridge, don't you worry about me.
JOAN. But I do.
VICTOR. But you mustn't. Cold lamb, glass of milk. I'll be all right. I'll come up in the morning. Bye-bye. Take care.

(JOAN *exits. They all shout good-bye.* VICTOR *moves to the kitchen door and waves off to them, then helps himself to a drink as he hears the car driving off.* SHIRLEY *enters up* R, *dressed as in her first entrance but without the crash helmet*)

SHIRLEY. Hullo.
VICTOR (*moving to her*) Hullo. Where's the bike?
SHIRLEY. In the summer-house, with my things.
VICTOR. Clever.

(*They hold hands*)

SHIRLEY. Let's lie in the garden and get deliciously brown.
VICTOR (*moving down* L; *laughing*) I'll be with you in two-and-a-half minutes. I'll just slip into something loose.

(SHIRLEY *blows Victor a kiss.* VICTOR *exits upstairs, laughing and singing*)

(*Off*) "I'm in the mood for love, simply because you're near me."

(SHIRLEY *starts to take off her jacket, then, getting a sudden naughty idea, exits up* R *to the garden.* JOAN *enters down* L, *gently calling Victor*)

JOAN. Victor.
VICTOR (*off; singing*) "Darling and when you're near me, I'm in the mood for love."

(JOAN *moves down* L, *then, getting a nice thought, exits to the kitchen.* VICTOR *enters down* L *in his dressing-gown, gently calls to Shirley, then exits up* L *to the garden, looking for her.* JOAN *enters from the kitchen with a tray set for lunch, puts it on the table down* C, *and exits happily to the kitchen.* SHIRLEY *enters up* R *in shorts or a bikini, sees the food, helps herself, and moves* R *to the fireplace.* JOAN *enters from the kitchen with champagne in an ice bucket. She sees Shirley.* VICTOR *enters up* L *and sees Shirley*)

Darling . . . (*He sees Joan*)

CURTAIN

FURNITURE AND PROPERTY LIST

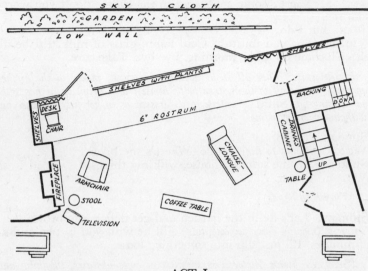

ACT I

On stage: Writing desk (up R) *On it:* ashtray, lighter, box of cigarettes, notepad, pencil. *On floor:* waste-paper basket
Desk chair
Drinks cabinet (L) *On it:* bottles of brandy, sherry, whisky, lime juice, vodka, gin, 2 sherry glasses, 4 brandy glasses, tumbler, bowl of crisps, ashtray
Coffee-table (C) *On it:* full cigarette box, ashtray, lighter, bowl of apples
Chaise-longue (LC) *On it:* magazines
Armchair (R) *On it:* copy of *The Times*
Stool (down R)
Television set (down R) *On top:* Radio Times, TV Times
Carpet
Window curtains

Off stage: Vase of roses (MARTIN)
Apron (MARTIN)
Crash helmet (SHIRLEY)
Rucksack and crash helmet (GILES)
Bottle of lager (GILES)
Teacloth (MARTIN)

ACT II

Strike: Dirty glasses

Set: Television set slightly on stage

Off stage: Cigarette and matches (GILES)
Book, glass of milk, plate with 3-decker sandwich (VICTOR)
Blanket and pillow (SHIRLEY)

Personal: VICTOR: watch

ACT III

Strike: Book, tumbler, plate

Set: Stool in original position
Pad and pencil back to desk
Cigarette ends in all ashtrays

Off stage: Tea towel and apron (MARTIN)
Rug (MILES)
Trolley with coffee, tea, milk, sugar, 4 cups and saucers, 4 plates,
4 knives, 4 teaspoons, toast-rack and toast, 4 napkins (MARTIN)
Tray with coffee-pot, milk jug, cup and saucer, spoon, plate,
knife, toast-rack and toast (MARTIN)
Duster (MARTIN)
Handbag (JOAN)
2 suitcases (JOAN)
Zip bag (MARTIN)
Tray with 2 champagne glasses, 2 knives, 2 forks, bowl of crisps,
bowl of salad, joint of lamb on chopping board (JOAN)
Champagne bottle in ice bucket (JOAN)

Personal: SHIRLEY: watch
MARTIN: purse with 4 half-crowns
VICTOR: 3 £5 notes

LIGHTING PLOT

Property fittings required: 3 electric oil lamps on brackets, standard lamp (R), table lamp (on drinks cabinet) wall bracket in hall

Interior. A living-room. The same scene throughout

THE APPARENT SOURCES OF LIGHT are: by day, french windows up L and up R; by night, brackets and lamps

THE MAIN ACTING AREAS are: down R, RC, up C, down C, LC, down L

ACT I. Morning

To open: Effect of morning light

No cues

ACT II. Night

To open: Lamp brackets, hall brackets and table lamp on

Cue 1   VICTOR switches on standard lamp   (Page 28)
         Snap on standard lamp

Cue 2   VICTOR starts to read   (Page 28)
         Fade to Black-Out

Cue 3   When ready   (Page 28)
         *Fade up to previous lighting, except that hall bracket and
             kitchen light remain out*

Cue 4   VICTOR switches off standard lamp   (Page 29)
         Snap out standard lamp

Cue 5   VICTOR switches off main lights   (Page 29)
         Snap out wall brackets

Cue 6   SHIRLEY switches off table lamp   (Page 30)
         Black-Out

Cue 7   VICTOR switches on main lights and table lamp   (Page 30)
         Snap on brackets, followed by table lamp

Cue 8   VICTOR switches on hall bracket   (Page 33)
         Snap on hall bracket

Cue 9   GILES switches off main lights and table lamp   (Page 34)
         Snap out brackets followed by table lamp

Cue 10   VICTOR switches on brackets   (Page 35)
           Snap on brackets

ACT III.   Morning

To open :   Room in darkness. Daylight effect outside closed window curtains

Cue 11   MARTIN draws curtains   (Page 39)
           Quick fade up to full daylight

EFFECTS PLOT

ACT II

ACT III

Printed in Great Britain by
Biddles Ltd, Guildford, Surrey